Learning from Imperfections: Building Datasets with Probabilistic Alignment of Handwritten Text

Georgia

Contents

1 Introduction   **1**

2 Background   **3**
   2.1 Shorthand and the Melin system   3
   2.2 The Astrid Lindgren code   4

3 Purpose, aims, and motivation   **6**

4 Theory   **9**
   4.1 Convolutional Neural Network   9
      4.1.1 Over-fitting   9
      4.1.2 The neuron   9
      4.1.3 Input   11
   4.2 Activation functions   11
      4.2.1 Layers   12
      4.2.2 Loss function   14
   4.3 Building the CNN   15
   4.4 Training and classification   15
   4.5 CNN's for feature extraction   15
   4.6 Edit distance   16

5 Related work   **18**
   5.1 Pyramidal histogram of characters   18
   5.2 Automatic Alignment of Handwritten Images and Transcripts for Train-
      ing Handwritten Text Recognition Systems   18
   5.3 Attribute CNNs for Word Spotting in Handwritten Documents   19

	5.4	Text alignment in early printed books combining deep learning and dynamic programming	19
	5.5	Unsupervised Word Clustering Using Deep Features	20
	5.6	Handwriting Recognition using CNN	20
6	**Data**		**22**
7	**Method**		**26**
	7.1	Pre-processing	26
	7.2	Feature extraction	27
	7.3	Similarity measuring	27
	7.4	Index matching	28
	7.5	Filling in the gaps	31
	7.6	Creating the data set	32
	7.7	Edit distance	34
	7.8	Parameters	34
		7.8.1 Fill distance	34
		7.8.2 Image neighbours	34
		7.8.3 Word neighbours	35
		7.8.4 Feature space max distance, image neighbours	35
		7.8.5 Feature space max distance, created data set	35
	7.9	Evaluation methods	36
8	**Delimitations**		**37**
	8.1	Word segmentation	37
9	**System structure**		**37**

10 Results   **40**

   10.1 CNN and feature extraction 40

   10.2 Visualisation of results on one page 43

   10.3 Improvements with data set creation 50

   10.4 Shorthand results 56

        10.4.1 Outtake from textbook on Melin shorthand 56

        10.4.2 Melin shorthand Wikipedia page 58

   10.5 Misalignment 60

11 Discussion   **62**

   11.1 CNN classification accuracy 62

   11.2 Results of index matching 63

   11.3 Line data and segmentation robustness 63

   11.4 The created data set 64

   11.5 Shorthand 65

   11.6 Misalignment 66

12 Conclusion   **68**

13 Future work   **69**

A Appendix A   **72**

1   Introduction

Analysing handwritten texts and creating data sets can facilitate research on languages and the analysis of authors works. Few handwritten works have word wise labelling or data sets associated with them. By creating an algorithm that can utilise only a word segmented image of a handwritten text and the transcript more works could be analysed.

Words can be added or removed while transcribing, to make sense of what the author has written. This causes information to get lost. As a result of this a data set cannot be created with good accuracy of data, since each word-image is not perfectly matched to each transcribed word.

Can an algorithm be created that will take only an image of handwritten text and a corresponding transcript and return a partial alignment and a data set?

The algorithm created for this book is intended to label images given only an image of word segmented handwritten text and a transcript of this text. For the algorithm to function some assumptions about the text must be fulfilled. These assumptions allow for several types of data being able to be analysed by the same algorithm. It is therefore not bound to a specific language. The two languages tested are English handwritten letters and Swedish short hand texts.

The word images must be able to be described by parameters extracted from a Convolutional Neural Network (CNN). This to determine what words look similar. The similarity of word images is what is used to create an alignment. The algorithm finds words that are common in the text and identifies these by the shape of the word image and its position on the page. It uses the features it creates for each image to return an alignment, linking words in the transcript to word images given the similarity of reoccurring words in the text. These words are added as labelled images to a data set. A labelled data set of word images subsequently grows with each page shown to the algorithm and is used to facilitate better alignments on future pages. This yields not only a probable alignment of words to word images on a page but also a data set of labelled words.

This problem is especially relevant for the analysis of shorthand text. Shorthand is a technique for handwriting efficiently, by eliminating the use of separate letters and combinations of letters to build words. Instead, a shorthand word is written using small twists and turns to represent sounds on a single line, resulting in one curved line representation of each word [22]. Because of this curved line representation, character segmentation is difficult. The curves overlap and have different lengths, and have by definition no separation. Because of this, the algorithm must learn each word as a whole, instead of learning the letters and building words, in the way a language is usually learnt.

There are several important works written in shorthand. To be able to analyse the important texts authors have left behind, written in shorthand, an algorithm may be created to be able to categorise word data at a large scale. The language-agnostic implementation though is not tailored specifically for shorthand, but rather for texts that carry the same limitations as shorthand texts. This is done by setting four assumptions on the text data. The algorithm is intended for data that fulfills these assumptions and for which word images can be described by the same features as English handwritten words.

A CNN is trained to classify word images of historical English texts. This trains the network to recognise important features from each word image to classify what word it corresponds to. This can then assign new unlabelled word images important features. The features are then used to describe how similar two word images are. If images are similar according to the CNN the images are considered probable to represent the same word. If two words look similar and happen to match the same word at, or close to, their respective indexes in the transcript, then the image can be labelled with a high probability. No knowledge of what each word image represents is needed beforehand, the algorithm will find and store labelled words as pages are provided to the algorithm.

2   Background

In this section some background is given to shorthand and projects related to this.

2.1   Shorthand and the Melin system

Shorthand is the act of writing in a language generally written with Latin characters in a more efficient way than what the regular Latin alphabet will allow. Through hundreds of years different authors have invented and refined new alphabets, systems and abbreviations to be able to write as quickly as possible [16].

Olof Melin learnt several shorthand systems invented for different languages and concluded that a new system, specialised for the characters and sounds of the Swedish language was needed. He authored a new alphabet and in 1892 he started teaching this new system. It soon became a success [16].

Figure 1 An example of shorthand representations of some Swedish words. Consonants are typically written from right to left and vowels left to right. This can be seen in the word "hy" where the "h" is represented by the line running from the top of the word in a diagonal line toward the bottom left. This line then continues into a "y" running in a curved line from left to right. The length of the line distinguishes the "y" from for example the "u" represented by a similar but shorter line in the middle of the following word "hur". The letter "r" in "hur" is represented by a small circle at the end of the line.

Melin's shorthand consists of words where each word is represented by a line. On this line each sound is represented by a curve. Each curve does not necessarily represent a letter, the representation of a word is instead sound-dependent. This is shown in figure 1.

Melin's shorthand is quick and efficient a nd r esults i n a c oncise t ext representation. This is achieved at the cost of legibility. Shorthand texts are only legible to those who are trained in shorthand themselves, even with a dictionary at hand [22]. This can be a challenge to the traditional word alignment methods, as data sets and dictionaries to reference are hard to come by. Even with a shorthand dictionary available, letters in a word would be difficult to separate because of the words' single-line nature. This results in a problem that requires a non-traditional approach to be solved. Finding shorthand data for testing of the algorithm proved difficult. As a result a small amount of shorthand text is manually segmented and used in testing.

The purpose of this book is to build an algorithm that relies on four assumptions that can be made for shorthand texts. These assumptions are described in section 3. The algorithm is trained and tested on English historical texts, for which the assumptions hold. A small amount of shorthand texts are tested to examine if the assumptions the algorithm relies on also hold for shorthand data.

2.2   The Astrid Lindgren code

The children's book author Astrid Lindgren is one of Sweden's most famous writers. Her books are seen as children's book classics. She wrote 41 chapter books in her lifetime, which lasted between 1907-2002. The amount of Astrid Lindgren books sold is calculated to a total of 165 million copies [4].

Astrid learnt Melin shorthand at her secretarial training at the Bar-Lock institute 1926–27. At the time Melin shorthand was standard practice in Sweden. Her writing style is sweeping and proportions are not particularly regarded. She also prefers to write out shorthand words rather than create her own abbreviations. Her books are written in shorthand, contained in large amounts of notebooks. Her notebooks are filled with pages upon pages of these small squiggles, and the notebooks have been inventoried and stored. [6]. These notebooks as well as letters she wrote and received, manuscripts for films a nd p lays, photos, posters and o ther i tems i s a p art of U NESCO M emory of the World Register [1].

This is strong proof of her influence, which i n itself j ustifies an alysing he r wo rks. In 2020 The Astrid Lindgren code, an interdisciplinary collaboration between Uppsala University and The Swedish Institute for Children's Books was initiated. The project's purpose is deciphering Astrid Lindgren's shorthand writing found in the previously mentioned notebooks. The purpose of the project is double, where the first part is to use handwritten text recognition (HTR) to access Lindgren's shorthand drafts and to use crowdsourcing to develop and refine the digital method. This project is set to run until the end of 2022. Responsible for the project is Malin Nauwerck [5]. Nauwerck (personal communication, 25 May 2021) describes how the project is intended to use crowdsourcing to create transcripts for Lindgrens shorthand notes, this data is then to be used to create algorithms to facilitate analysis of further works by Lindgren.

The project is an inspiration for the specific implementation of the algorithm in this project that builds on certain limitations in the data. This project is independent and intended to be useful for several languages, most useful for those who share specific limitations. The limitations on the data are detailed in section 2.1 and the purpose is discussed further in section 3.

3 Purpose, aims, and motivation

To be able to analyse data effectively it must be structured in some way. The purpose
of this book is to create an algorithm that can build a labelled data set as well as return
a probable alignment between word images on a page and a transcript for some words.
This is intended as an aid to analyse single pages or analyse the language on a higher
level for a larger amount of data. The purpose is to align some words on each page, and
use these to create better alignments in the future, this is denoted as a partial alignment
of a page.

To manually annotate books written in shorthand not only must the person annotating
have the skill of reading shorthand, but they must also use this knowledge to annotate
each word. This would be hard work even with all the help and software available. In
the case of some shorthand documents, the data available is images of handwritten pages
and the transcript of these pages. The purpose of the algorithm is to use only pages and
transcripts as inputs and result in not only a partial alignment but a data set for future
training. With this approach, large amounts of data could be effectively analysed and a
data set developed to facilitate future work on the language.

The purpose of this algorithm is not to create a system that will align exclusively shorthand, but rather create an algorithm that is built on a few assumptions. These assumptions can be made for shorthand, but also for the English language, as well as for other
types of data. The algorithm will be tested for performance on data that fulfil the assumptions, and conclusions of the efficiency of the algorithm drawn from the results of
these tests. The data used in this project is separate parts of the IAM data set. Results
will also be presented for a very small set of shorthand data. This to show preliminary
results showing if the assumptions that allow the algorithm to function, also hold for
shorthand data.

There are a fair few Optical Character Recognition (OCR) and alignment methods available, a few related to handwritten text recognition are outlined in section 5. Shorthand
writing has a few caveats in regards to OCR and alignment. Since this is a non-trivial
problem that regular algorithms are not adapted for a new approach must be taken. Below some assumptions that can be made for this type of handwriting are outlined, to use
as the pillars for the algorithm to lie on.

The purpose is to create a language-agnostic algorithm that only relies on four assumptions:

1. The transcript is fairly similar to the page layout, with only occasional added or
   dropped words and the total misalignment between the transcript and the hand-

written text does not exceed a few words per page.

2. Each word has a different visual representation and two instances of the same word will have similar visual representations.

3. Words must be segmented, which presents the requirement of separate words or words that are possible to segment by some rule.

4. The text must be fairly uniform, some words must be reoccurring on each page, or quite a few common words can be annotated manually.

To be noted is that this approach is language and representation agnostic. There must be no translation dictionary or knowledge about the visual representation of any given word, it is agnostic on a word level. On a page-level, the transcript must exist for the algorithm to function. The algorithm is intended for the alignment of data without the need for any re-training. A machine learning model is used to extract a feature description of each image, no additional training of this model is to be required for new data. Some parameters ought to be adjusted for each new type of data the algorithm is provided.

As the algorithm is provided pages, the intention is to build a created data set of labelled images. The information from this ever-growing data set is to be used to create more confident alignments. This will render the first assumption as described above less influential, allowing for larger misalignment between the word images on a page and the transcript.

Finding an annotated and labelled shorthand data set proved to be difficult. Some data could be found for testing, requiring manual word segmentation. For better analysis, the IAM data set will be used for training of the CNN and a large part of the results. This is free to use and contains pages of text segmented into lines and words, all annotated in metadata. This data will be used in training the network utilised for feature extraction, as described in detail in section 4.1. A few pages not seen in training are used to evaluate the results of the algorithm and the alignment, to be able to evaluate the algorithms strength in alignment and data set creation. A small manually annotated data set of shorthand data can then be tested to investigate if this data shares some attributes, such as the CNN being able to group similar shorthand words in the feature space, as well as if the shorthand data has words reoccurring in the text. Given this information, assumptions can be made about the result of the algorithm on larger amounts of shorthand data.

The intention is to create a proof of concept of an algorithm relying on a few assumptions outlined above. This algorithm should only accept pages of handwritten words and transcripts of these pages and create a probable alignment and data set of annotated

words. The created data set should grow with the number of pages and transcripts provided. The data in the created data set should be correctly labelled and this data set
should be utilised to be able to make alignments on increasing percentages of the page.

4   Theory

In this section, a few important scientific concepts are described. These concepts are what the algorithm is built upon.

4.1   Convolutional Neural Network

Convolutional neural networks (CNN's) are based upon the idea of a large network built on neurons that each carry out a simple calculation. A parallel can be drawn to the neurons in a brain.

A CNN can be used to find patterns in images, for which one use case is classification. In classification, the network is provided many samples of content and labels describing the content in some way. The content information will be threaded through the network and the many neurons will find patterns and connect these to the label of the content. It will eventually be able to determine the label of a new piece of content with some accuracy [12]. Training a CNN as a classifier of word images results in a network that learns to distinguish words from one another.

4.1.1   Over-fitting

Over-fitting is a side effect of training the CNN and must be avoided. This occurs when the CNN learns the training data too well. Rather than learning the features connected with a specific label it instead learns what the correct answer is by heart. This will give it a high accuracy in training, but when new data is provided the network accuracy will decline. To combat over-fitting several measures are taken. Dropout layers, as well as pooling layers, are added to the model. Layers are described in section 4.2.1. It is important to test the network on data it has not seen in training to evaluate results. This confirms the network has learnt the features instead of the training data. Testing on new data is commonly done by splitting data into training, test and validation data [17].

4.1.2   The neuron

The CNN is built upon neurons utilising convolution. A neuron is a small building block with a basic principle, it computes a simple mathematical computation, taking inputs and using these to mathematically compute an output. The input can be a large number of values, such as pixels in an image. Each input, each value, is referred to as x_n and each weight the neuron remembers and learns by is referred to as w_n [17].

Convolution refers to the linear computation using internal weights in the neuron and its inputs. Convolution is then carried out efficiently using the mathematical concept of convolution over a square grid or image. The output z is defined as $z = w_1x_1 + w_2x_2 + w_3x_3 + w_4x_4 + ... + w_mx_m$ for m inputs. The w_n represents the weights connected with the neuron and x_n the inputs [9].

For each neuron the output z, which due to the nature of convolution is a real number, is augmented by a function referred to as the activation function for the specified neuron. The output of this augmentation will be referred to as y and the activation function itself as $f(z)$. The activation functions used in this book are described further in the following parts of this section. One common activation function is ReLU, which converts the output to a positive value, converting negative values of z to 0 [12].

The neuron is visualised in figure 2 where the computations described above are shown.

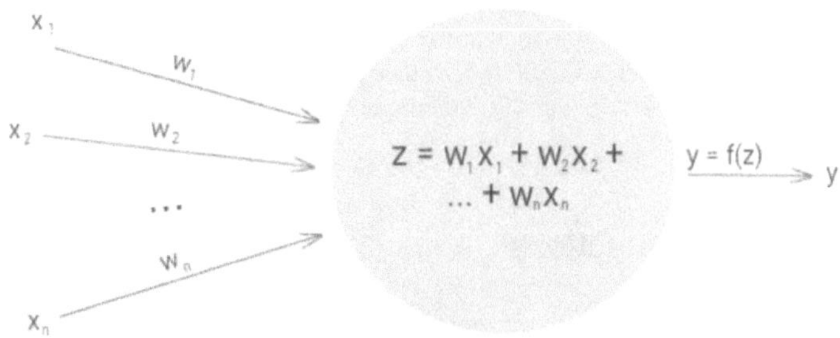

Figure 2 A visualisation of the neuron, the building block of the CNN. It takes an array of inputs and the weights connected to the neuron and convolutes these. It then calculates the output using an activation function.

These neurons build the basis of the entire CNN, the convolutional layers. The weights associated with each neuron is what stores information. These weights are also the variables in the network and what "learns" from each input the network is given [17].

4.1.3 Input

Each image in the input data can be described as a number of pixel values as each image will have a set amount of pixels and each pixel will have a value of some sort. An image with 224×224 pixels in RGB-color will have three dimensions, $224 \times 224 \times 3$ where the three represent the colour value of red, green and blue respectively, to describe the colour of the pixel. Using the same reasoning a black and white image will have three dimensions defined as $224 \times 224 \times 1$ as the colour is a measure of lightness to darkness on a scale. This is what is used as input to the CNN and what the network makes its calculations upon.

The input data must be split into training data, for the network to learn from. Validation data, for the network to test its correctness on, and test data, to test the functionality of the algorithm. These data sets should be separated [17].

The labels can also be pre-processed to facilitate better learning for the network. One example of such pre-processing is one-hot-encoding. This refers to the act of translating a set amount of labels into a common description type. This is done by creating an array with the length of the number of classes to be encoded. Each one of these labels is then assigned a position in this array. To describe a label the array is set to "1" in the position associated with that label, and "0" in all other array positions [12]. For example, if the labels were to be "A", "B", and "C" their one hot encoded representations could be $[1, 0, 0]$, $[0, 1, 0]$, $[0, 0, 1]$.

4.2 Activation functions

An activation function is used on the output of each layer to augment the outputs of the layer as explained in 4.1.2. In practice, two activation functions are used in most cases, Sigmoid and Rectified Linear Unit (ReLU) [17]. In this project, ReLU and SoftMax will be used, described below. ReLU is considered standard practice for CNN's used for image classification [17].

The ReLU activation function is defined as $f(z) = max(0, z)$ where z is the output of the layer. This in practice removes all negative output values [12]. The function is shown in figure 3.

The SoftMax activation function can be used toward the end of a model for classification into a fairly large amount of classes [13]. It is defined as:

$$f(\vec{z})_i = \frac{e^{z_i}}{\sum_{j=1}^{k} e^{z_j}}$$

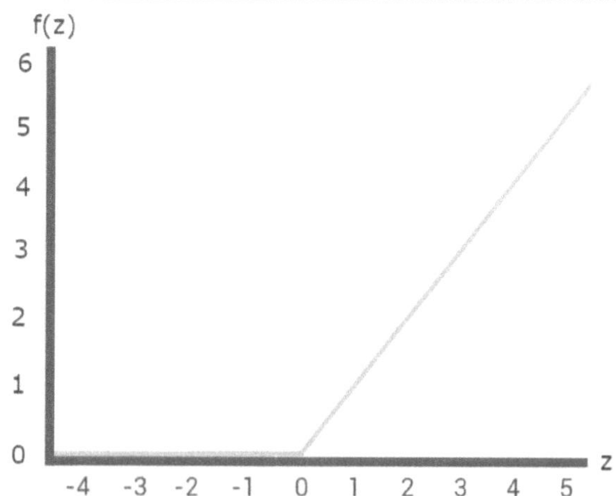

Figure 3 A visualisation of the ReLu activation function augmenting the output of the neurons.

Where k is the amount of classes for the data to be classified into. $\vec{z}$ is the input vector, as described in section 4.1.2 as z. e represents the regular exponential function.

The SoftMax activation function returns a vector of values that sum to 1, therefore following a probability distribution [10]. The labels one hot encoded, which is described in section 7.1. By having the labels defined in this way the output can be used to resolve the most probable label, enabling for classification into many classes [24] [13].

4.2.1 Layers

A CNN is built using layers, these layers are stacked to give the network some properties. Such properties can be recognising images or being less prone to over-fitting. Layers often used to build a CNN are convolutional layers, pooling layers, flatten layers, dropout layers and fully connected layers [12]. These will all be explained in this section.

The convolutional layers are vital for a CNN to be able to recognise features. It can be explained as a filter, this is called a kernel and is a small matrix, in this project 3×3 or 5×5, which can be seen as representing pixel values in a very small 3×3 or 5×5 image. This filter is then convolved with an area of the image, pixel by pixel. The filter is then advanced along the image by a stride. The stride is the number of pixels the filter is moved along the image at each step. Because of the nature of convolution the result of each convolution across the image is a single number in each pixel [12]. These convolutional layers are built upon the neurons, described in section 4.1.2, and are the most important part of a CNN.

Another important layer type, to combat over-fitting, is pooling layers. These are often placed in between the convolutional layers. Pooling layers downsample the image representation. The purpose of this is reducing the parameters, as a reduction of parameters often results in a reduction of over-fitting [17]. A pooling-layer is a filter which often down-samples the image by using a stride of 2, moving across the image and sampling a 2×2 area. It does this by taking the maximum value from this pixel area. This will reduce a $N \times N$-image to $\frac{N}{2} \times \frac{N}{2}$-image [9]. This process is shown in figure 4.

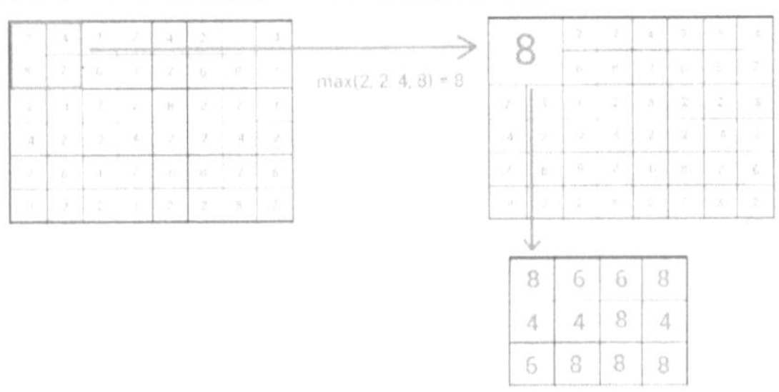

Figure 4 This image shows the process of down-sampling an image, visualised as a matrix of pixel values, using a max-pooling layer.

The flatten layer acts by reshaping the input into a 1-dimensional vector. As described in section 4.1.3 the input images consist of 3-dimensions. Transforming the 3-dimensional input to the layer into a 1-dimensional output prepares for the next layer, which is fully connected [12]. It also facilitates a concise representation of each input image.

Dense, or fully-connected, layers of neurons have connections between all neurons in one layer and all neurons in the next. In figure 5 this is shown. These are often added toward the end of the model [12].

Dropout layers are inserted to avoid over-fitting. In dropout layers neurons chosen at random are dropped in training [7]. Different neurons are removed each iteration effectively resulting in the model training on slightly different networks [17].

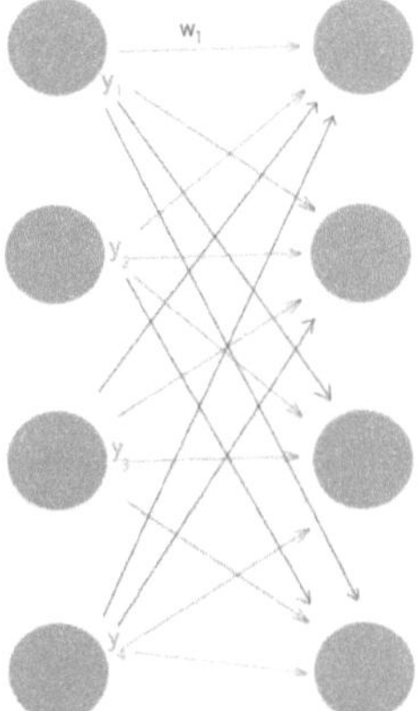

Figure 5 A visualisation of a fully connected layer, connecting two layers of neurons, one layer of neuron shown on the left in blue and one on the right in green. The output from each neuron in the first layer is sent to each neuron in the next. Each neuron and its function is described in section 4.1.2 and shown in figure 2.

How these layers are used to build a CNN is shown later in this section, in subsection 4.3.

4.2.2 Loss function

As described in section 4.1.2 the weights associated with each neuron is where the information learnt is stored. These weights must be optimised for as correct of a classification as possible, to create a network that learns. The optimisation must be defined by some measure, this measure is called a loss function. The loss function is used to evaluate the divergence of a prediction from the correct label. There are many loss functions, where a few are adapted for classification. One of these is binary cross-entropy, a measure of divergence from a class, optimised for binary classification, which is classification into two classes. As the divergence increases, the loss function further increases the loss value. This has then been expanded into categorical cross-entropy, which is based on the same principle, for an increased amount of classes [17].

4.3   Building the CNN

In this section, the concepts described above are used to build a CNN.

A standard CNN architecture consists of three types of layers. These types are convolutional layers and pooling layers as well as at least one fully connected layer. To create a CNN several convolutional layers and pooling layers are added, stacked on one another [12]. Each convolutional layer can be seen as filters. The filter will teach itself to find a set of features, examples of features are patterns, edges or bigger objects [18].

Fully connected, or Dense, layers are added toward the end of the model. This connects all the neurons in the input to the layer to all the neurons in the output, as described in section 4.2.1. The output layer is a fully connected layer, facilitating classification using SoftMax as the activation function, this described further in section 4.1 [18].

4.4   Training and classification

After the model has been built it must be trained, to be able to learn from the data. The network is provided images of words that each have a one-hot encoded label associated with them. The network uses the images as input data to the first layer of neurons, which will convolve the input values with its weights. As the weights are updated, the network will learn how to classify each type of data into one of the classes provided. When the network has finished training it should be able to classify a new image belonging to one of the pre-defined classes with high accuracy.

4.5   CNN's for feature extraction

A crucial part of the algorithm that is later developed in this book is the ability to measure the similarity between two word images that the algorithm has never seen before. To do this all words must be described by some features to be compared. By training a CNN to recognise word images the network learns how to describe each image. It then uses this description to be able to make a correct classification during training. By extracting this description of an image, which the CNN has created, the features can be compared and analysed [21]. The act of extracting the parameter description for any image is equivalent to simply extracting the weights from the last layer of neurons of the CNN after using the image in question as the input. These weights are, due to the flatten layer, a one dimensional vector. This can be viewed as the images position in the feature space, where the distance to other image features define similarity. In figure 6 an example 2D feature space is shown. In reality, the feature space referred to in this book consists of many dimensions which would be far more difficult to visualise. The figure should only be considered a way to visualise what is referred to as proximity in the feature space, which is equivalent to the measure of similarity of word images.

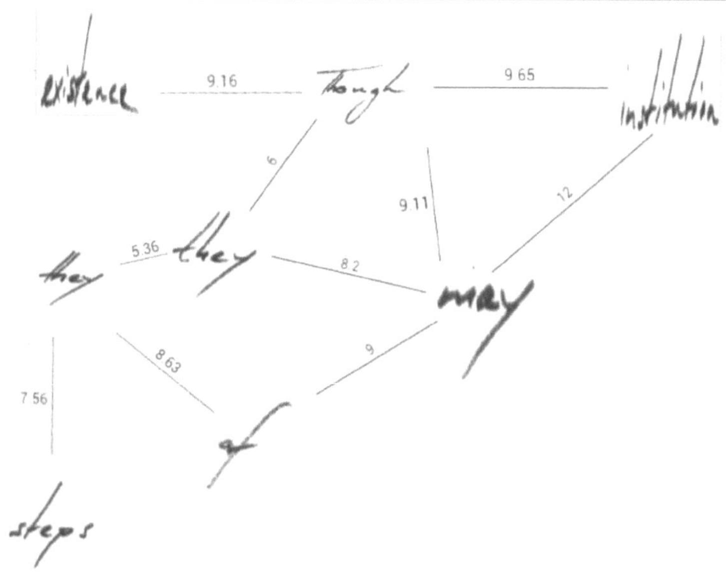

Figure 6 This figure attempts to show the characteristics of a word feature space, visualising word images as a graph with edges and weights representing distances between some of the words. The features each word receives are used to calculate the difference between words, which can be seen as the distance or weights in this graph. Note the proximity of the words "they" and "they", two similar words. Also note the distance between "Though" and "institution", two fairly different words. Not all distances are shown, for clarity.

4.6   Edit distance

Levenshtein distance is a measure of the difference between two strings. It describes the minimum number of changes it would take to change one string into another. The changes are defined as insertion, deletion and substitution. An illustrative example of a Levenshtein distance between two strings is that the distance between "bread" and "broad" is 1, a simple substitution of e vs o [19].

For simplicity of implementation, a deletion can be described as an addition of a null character in the other string. For example, the Levenshtein distance between "chat" and "cat" is 1, a deletion of the character h, which can correspond to an addition of a null character in the other string, resulting in the strings "chat" and "c_at".

Edit distance can be seen as a generalised version of Levenshtein distance. Edit distance is the number of edits required to turn one sentence or piece of text into another. This can be modified to take into account the similarity of words in the text, defined by Levenshtein distance. This means similar words are prioritised matches while aligning the two texts.

More about edit distance can be read in [11] on page 406.

5   Related work

In the following section some important related research projects are described as well as the lessons learnt from previous research.

5.1   Pyramidal histogram of characters

In [24] Sudholt and Fink attempt to carry out word spotting using a CNN to extract features. These sets of features are denoted as Pyramidial Histograms Of Characters, PHOC'S. Using this PHOC representation they train a network that has an accuracy that surpasses what they denote as "state of the art" results [24].

The way this is done in [24] is by giving each word image label a PHOC-representation relating to the existence and position of letters in the label and training a CNN to recognise these representations as labels for word images.

Some of the concepts can be translated and used for word alignment in shorthand, the act of using a CNN for feature extraction, taking a picture as input and receiving a feature vector as the output, is relevant to this project. The PHOC representation of the label could be relevant if the CNN was to be trained on shorthand data, but as shorthand data is not available this approach is only partly suitable for the task at hand [24].

5.2   Automatic Alignment of Handwritten Images and Transcripts for Training Handwritten Text Recognition Systems

In [20] Toselli and Sánchez describe an algorithm they created for alignment of handwritten text. They use only the transcript of a page the image of this page. They segment by lines and carry out decoding of each line image given by Handwritten Text Recognition based on Hidden Markov Models. This to create a joint representation of the lines in the transcript and the lines in the image. Using this representation a most probable alignment between each line image and line in a transcript can be found.

This is useful to this book as the concept of being able to align texts without using training data is relevant. The largest issue that this book faces as opposed to the authors of [20] is that the data this book is aimed to be able to align can not be assumed to be segmented by lines. The representation of each image is adapted to a sequence of words that cannot be translated into a representation of each word with as favourable results.

5.3   Attribute CNNs for Word Spotting in Handwritten Documents

In [23] Sudholt and Fink create a system related to the one described in 5.1, as a continuation of their previous work. They use this system to carry out word spotting in handwritten documents by projecting both words and word images into a shared PHOC-space.

This too is built upon the idea of PHOC's as a label representation. They then use a CNN to place each word image in a feature space. The feature space representation of images to be able to measure similarity is related to the work done in this book. This is an effective way of measuring the similarity of images without having to show the specified image in training. What they refer to as the "attribute space" is similar to what is referred to as the "feature space" in this book. The labels, words from the transcripts, are then projected into the same feature space.

This paper serves as a good concept to base this book on, but it shares some issues with the paper described in section 5.1 as they are closely related. The CNN must still be trained on data with PHOC-labelled relevant data, which in the case of this book would be shorthand data, not available. The need for training on relevant labelled data is related to the fact that both pure words and word images are projected into the same space, meaning they must be related in some way. The method proposed in this book circumvents this issue by only giving word images a measure of similarity, and finding an alignment given similar words, regardless of the representation of the label.

5.4   Text alignment in early printed books combining deep learning and dynamic programming

In [8] Ziran et al. discuss an approach for text alignment in early printed books using deep learning. The authors create a system that finds landmark words. They define landmark words as five common and easily classified words which are found with good accuracy to align the text by. They use the "longest common subsequence" in combination with landmark words to align the text. This is an approach in theory similar to the type of alignment carried out in this project. In reality, the constraints are larger on the data this project is intended for. In [8] not only is the text printed, which makes word segmentation far more trivial since the lines are well separated. More importantly for the alignment, each line break in the image matches the transcripts line break. This means it is simply a game of finding what line of word images corresponds to what transcript line.

Since the constraints on the data sets for this book are harder than in [8] this approach can be seen as an inspiration, from which we can extract important concepts, such as keyword alignment. Keyword alignment is inadvertently used in this book since words belonging to the 20 classes the network is trained on will be more easily recognised for English texts. The difference can be seen in the fact that because of the use of parameter descriptions all words have a set of parameters, as opposed to a subset of the words belonging to some keyword class.

5.5   Unsupervised Word Clustering Using Deep Features

In [14] Kurkarni et al. carry out a feature extraction using a CNN. They use these features for unsupervised clustering of word images. This is done on Indian scripts. The authors find issues carrying out optical character recognition (OCR) on these texts, not unlike the issues in word alignment in shorthand. The main issue these types of data share is that character segmentation is non-trivial, making it difficult to use standard OCR techniques. This means the shape of the word has to stand alone, regardless of the characters it consists of.

The method the authors use to find an "artificial ground truth" is not unlike the one utilised in this book. They use an edge responsive untrained CNN is used as a feature extractor. This serves as an inspiration for this project since the feature extraction for the principle of finding images of words that have a similar shape is an important part of aligning the text. They then perform a graph connected component analysis. This is where the two projects diverge, because of the structure of data available. In their case, the data consists of Indian scripts that can be manually annotated and the clusters can be assigned a label [14]. Since this approach requires annotated data it cannot be directly translated to this project. The difference is in principle the difference between word clustering and word alignment.

5.6   Handwriting Recognition using CNN

In the project described at [2] Reddy shows a system for author recognition on the IAM data set, the same data set used for training in this project. The author designs a CNN for recognising the handwriting of handwritten words and uses this to classify new words into one of 20 classes, each one representing a different author. Since this network was designed for recognising handwritten words it was deemed relevant for the design of the CNN in this project. This architecture was an inspiration for the specific architecture of the CNN in this project even though the end purpose and the classification is intended for entirely different class types.

6 Data

The IAM handwriting database is a data set free to use for non-commercial research purposes. It contains 1539 pages of scanned text 115320 segmented and labelled words as well as labelled sentences, text lines and author information from the 657 authors [15]. The image of a page including its transcript data is shown in figure 7 more pages are shown in appendix A. A small part of the corresponding metadata is shown in 8.

The pages are in the format of PNG images with 256 grey levels and are scanned with a resolution of 300dpi. One such page is shown in figure 7. The data is segmented into words and each word is assigned a label that can then be used in training.

The IAM data set classifies punctuation marks in the same fashion it classifies words. In this book all labelled and segmented parts of the data set are referred to as words, this includes punctuation marks.

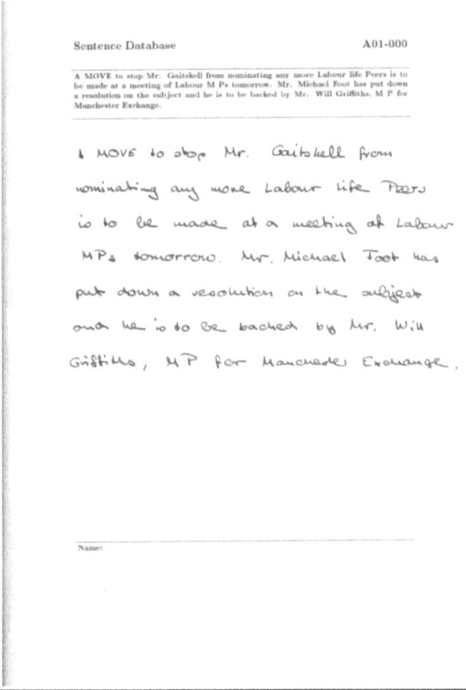

Sentence Database   A01-000

A MOVE to stop Mr. Gaitskell from nominating any more Labour life Peers is to
be made at a meeting of Labour M Ps tomorrow. Mr. Michael Foot has put down
a resolution on the subject and he is to be backed by Mr. Will Griffiths, M P for
Manchester Exchange.

A MOVE to stop Mr. Gaitskell from
nominating any more Labour life Peers
is to be made at a meeting of Labour
MPs tomorrow. Mr. Michael Foot has
put down a resolution on the subject
and he is to be backed by Mr. Will
Griffiths, MP for Manchester Exchange.

Name:

Figure 7 An example of a page from the IAM handwriting database, which is used for examples in the book and the testing of the algorithm. The page in the figure is a01-000u, written by the author represented who has the alias "u". At the top of the image the transcript is shown, and below the handwritten text is shown.

19	a01-000u-00-00	ok	154	408	768	27	51	AT	A
20	a01-000u-00-01	ok	154	507	766	213	48	NN	MOVE
21	a01-000u-00-02	ok	154	796	764	70	50	TO	to
22	a01-000u-00-03	ok	154	919	757	166	78	VB	stop
23	a01-000u-00-04	ok	154	1185	754	126	61	NPT	Mr.
24	a01-000u-00-05	ok	154	1438	746	382	73	NP	Gaitskell
25	a01-000u-00-06	ok	154	1896	757	173	72	IN	from
26	a01-000u-01-00	ok	156	395	932	441	100	VBG	nominating
27	a01-000u-01-01	ok	156	901	958	147	79	DTI	any
28	a01-000u-01-02	ok	156	1112	958	208	42	AP	more
29	a01-000u-01-03	ok	156	1400	937	294	59	NN	Labour
30	a01-000u-01-04	ok	156	1779	932	174	63	NN	life
31	a01-000u-01-05	ok	156	2008	933	237	70	NNS	Peers
32	a01-000u-02-00	ok	157	408	1106	65	70	BEZ	is
33	a01-000u-02-01	ok	157	541	1118	72	54	TO	to
34	a01-000u-02-02	ok	157	720	1114	113	63	BE	be
35	a01-000u-02-03	ok	157	916	1136	281	46	VBN	made
36	a01-000u-02-04	ok	157	1281	1117	80	59	IN	at
37	a01-000u-02-05	ok	157	1405	1140	64	35	AT	a
38	a01-000u-02-06	ok	157	1544	1115	339	96	NN	meeting
39	a01-000u-02-07	ok	157	1936	1106	91	74	INO	of

Figure 8 An example of a few lines of word-metadata from the page in figure 7. The initial serial number on each line carries information about content and author, which together make up a page. The following characters on the line carry information about the position of the word on the page as well as the label of the word. Not all annotated words are shown in the figures.

The strength of the IAM data set is its size and its versatile and well-annotated nature. This facilitates a wide array of use cases. As seen in section 5.6 the data can be used to train a machine learning model to recognise authors by their handwriting. It can also be used to classify images.

In this project, the data set is used to train a CNN for classification of some common words. The data set contains a variation of handwriting and a large number of words. The versatility of the data is shown in 9. This is required to not specialise in a specific pattern of a word, but to recognise the general shape.

Other data used in testing is shorthand data. This is found through a textbook for Melin shorthand where the data is pre-processed to remove the yellow background and the transcript is manually created. Another page is found through the Wikipedia page for

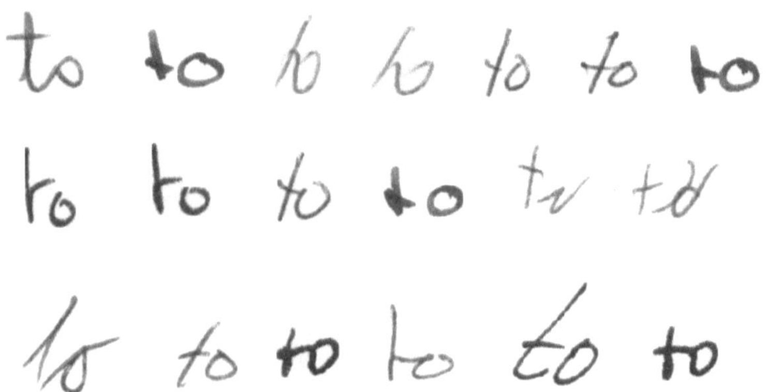

Figure 9 This figure illustrates the variation in the data set. It shows randomly selected images of the word "to" from the IAM data set.

Melin shorthand, where an example page and its corresponding transcript is found. Both of these pages are word segmented manually. The pre-processing for all data described in this section is described in 7.1.

7   Method

In the following section the algorithm will be outlined and important concepts described in detail. In section 7.8 the parameters used by the algorithm are listed and described.

7.1   Pre-processing

Because of the format of the data set the only pre-processing required on the IAM data set was rescaling of the images to a common size. In a real-life use case pre-processing in the form of enhancing the contrast between the characters and the background is required. This is carried out on the small amount of shorthand data tested in section 10.4. On this page pre-processing was needed to increase the contrast between the background, a yellowed book page, and the characters. This was done by converting the image to black and white and adding an adaptive threshold, which converted low pixel values (light areas) to white and high pixel values (dark areas) to black. This is done by taking a neighbourhood of $67x67$ pixels and calculating a threshold value for this area. This is then used to transform a pixel to either black or white, depending on if the value reaches the threshold or not. Word segmentation and transcription was done manually for 41 words.

To be able to use the IAM data set to train a CNN to handle classification not all labels can be chosen. In this project 20 classes, or labels, are used, and are chosen to be the 20 most common words in the data set used for training. These labels are then one-hot encoded. This was required for the SoftMax output layer of the model. These concepts are described further in section 4.1.

The part of the IAM data set that is used for training and validation has a size of 8047 images and their corresponding labels. The data is split into training, validation and test data using untouched pages. The training data of 7047 labelled images are used to train the network to recognise word shapes and classify them. 1000 labelled words are used for validation, which is a measure that can show if over-fitting occurs as described in 4.1.1. The last part of the data is a few pages taken from parts of the data set not used in training to use for testing of the algorithm. This to make sure the CNN has not been trained to recognise these specific images.

7.2   Feature extraction

To find the difference between two word images the images must be parameterised so a distance measure can be defined. The feature extraction was done through a CNN as outlined in 4.5. This CNN was trained on the IAM data set, using 7047 labelled word images and was trained as a standard classifier on 20 classes. These classes consisted of the 20 most common words in this data. The results of the CNN tested as a classifier for 20 classes are shown in section 10.1 and evaluated in 11.1. The network structure is shown in figure 10. The loss function used was categorical cross-entropy.

The features of each image are represented as a 256 long vector of values, describing the word image by some numerical features. Similarity of features is viewed as similarity of the word images, making it possible to identify several instances of the same word in a handwritten text.

To extract the features of each word image the weights of the last fully connected layer, a dense layer, are extracted and used as features representing the image used as input. These weights are received as a 256 long vector of numbers, which can be seen as the position of the picture in the feature space. This is described further in 4.5.

7.3   Similarity measuring

Finding images for which the parameter descriptions are close in the feature space is important, and is used to be able to determine similar words. This similarity between words is then used to determine labels for reoccurring words on the page, without using a data set to refer to.

Close neighbours in the feature space are deemed to have a high probability of representing the same word. This probability is then taken into account when determining the corresponding word in the transcript. Each word image is assigned a few neighbouring words in the feature space, the amount set as a parameter. The proximity measure used is Euclidean distance and each word is given a distance to every other word, the closest words are deemed as neighbours, given in order of proximity. These neighbours are, as described thoroughly in section 7.2 considered to have a similar representation by the CNN and therefore deemed more likely to represent the same word. Important to note is that all word images are given feature space neighbours, but not all words will have several instances.

Similarly to above, each word in the transcript is identified by its index and the word at that position. This is deemed the most probable label to word images at that same

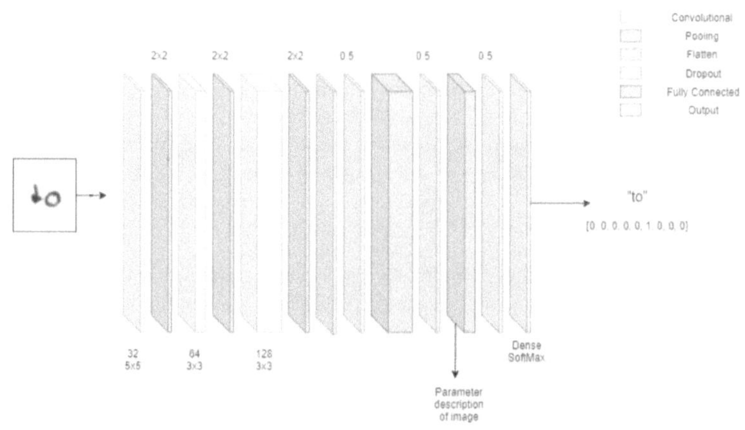

Figure 10 The CNN architecture, beginning with a convolutional layer with 32 filters and a 5x5 kernel, followed by a pooling layer. The model finishes with 20 outputs (9 shown in image), one for each class. The outputs are reached through a SoftMax activation function on a dense layer. The CNN is trained as a classifier for 20 classes. The layers are explained more thoroughly in section 4.1. Each of the convolutional layers is associated with a ReLU activation function. The last fully connected layer is from which features are extracted. This layer is where the parameter description of each image is extracted from, which is then used to compare the similarity of word images.

index of the word images. Associated with each word are also four additional words, the two preceding the word in question and the two following it in the transcript. These words are also used to determine probable matches. Using this technique tolerance for added or removed words becomes higher than if no neighbours in the transcript were considered.

7.4   Index matching

This section describes a vital part of the algorithm, the part that matches words on a page to each other and subsequently to words in the transcript, effectively labelling the words. This will be referred to as index matching. The data set described in section 7.6

is not used in this specific part of the algorithm. Index matching is instead used to build the data set, given only a handwritten page and a transcript. The words found by this method are referred to as landmark words.

Each word image is given a few image neighbours in the feature space as outlined in section 7.3. Each word has a few word image neighbours and each word also has a corresponding index in the transcript where the words are likely to be transcribed. Each word image, including each neighbour, has also been given a number of transcribed words that are adjacent to the probable location of the transcribed word in the text, ranked in order of adjacency to the index match, to adjust for misalignment.

The theory, as described more thoroughly in 9 can be described as that the most probable scenario is that each word-image corresponds to the word in the transcript at the matching index or close to it. This is an assumption made of the data, as described in section 3 assumption 1. By inspecting the corresponding places in the transcript for the words that are visually similar a conclusion can be drawn of which word it is probable to correspond to. A word is stored as the most probable match, given that one is found. This is then used in subsequent iterations as the neighbours to that word image have a label to refer to.

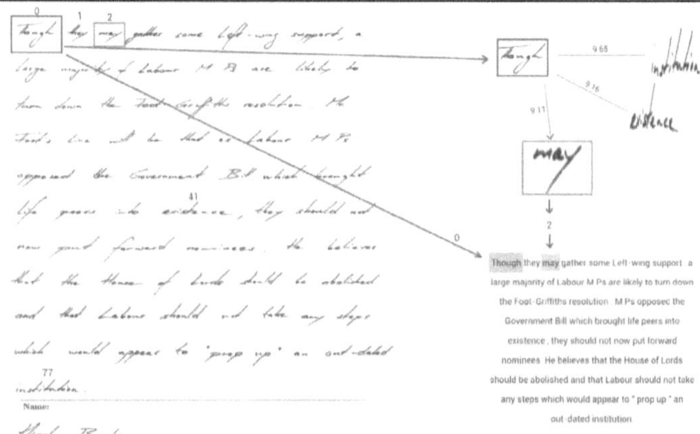

Figure 11 This figure illustrates the algorithms first word matching steps. Inspecting the word image at index 0, the word is outlined in green, both in the handwritten text and the transcript at the bottom right. The top right illustrates the image in a simplified "feature space" which contains three other word images, also placed in the feature space and their corresponding Euclidean distances from the word in green. The closest neighbour (in blue) is considered probable to represent the same word and is used as an indicator for where the word could be transcribed, at index 2. Since "though" does not show up at index 2 in the transcript no match is considered found and the next word is inspected. For simplicity the figure only shows the match at the exact index. All parameters used are outlined in section 7.8.

The theory can in simple terms be described as the assumption that if the word "book" is found in several places on the page the images will be similar and therefore be neighbours in the feature space. If when looking at the corresponding indexes in the transcript for both these words and the word found there is also "book" then it can be assumed that both of these images in fact represent the word "book" and words in the transcript and those words can be deemed aligned and subsequently saved as landmark words.

Words that are considered matches and are given a label are saved as reference matches. This creates the data set of labelled word images which can be referred to in subsequent iterations. By using this iterative method the algorithm will accumulate a set of labelled words which can be seen as keywords, to anchor the text by, creating better matches that are more robust to misalignment of the texts, as it does not refer to indexes.

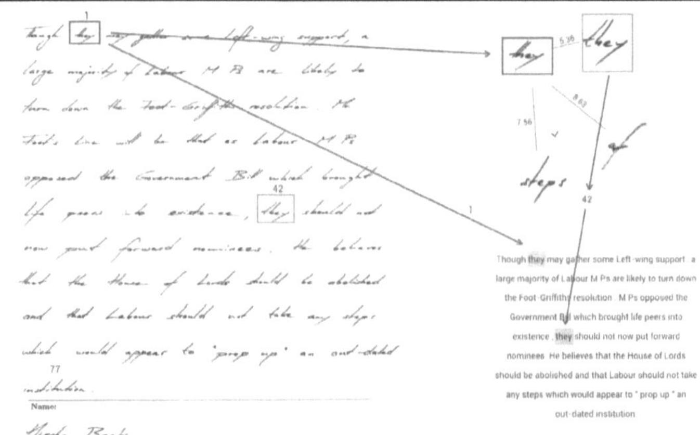

Figure 12 This figure illustrates the algorithms first word matching steps. Inspecting the word image at index 1, the word is outlined in green, both in the handwritten text and the transcript at the bottom right. The top right illustrates the image in a simplified "feature space" which contains three other word images, also placed in the feature space and their corresponding Euclidean distances from the word in green. The closest neighbour (in blue) is considered probable to represent the same word and is used as an indicator for where the word could be transcribed, at index 42. For simplicity the figure only shows the match at the exact index, in reality, the adjacent transcribed words are also taken into account to adjust for misalignment. Since "they" is shown at index 1 and 42 in the transcript the word at index 1 is labelled "they" and added to the data set.

7.5   Filling in the gaps

After finding landmark words in the image, the subsequent step is to inspect the interval between the landmark words. Assuming the space is small enough, and the number of word-images found in the space between landmark word images corresponds to the number of words in the transcript between the landmark words these gaps can be filled with some certainty. If these gaps equal one another each transcribed word is considered the label of the corresponding word-image within the space. As this gap size grows the risk of both an insertion and a deletion of words occurring within the same gap increases. This would lead to the number of words matching but the words being mislabelled. Since mislabelling images will cause a ripple effect of issues down the line this should be avoided and the gap size should therefore be kept relatively low and is used as a parameter. The words in the gaps are considered confirmed, and no difference is made between the words found by filling in gaps and words found by index matching. In this way, less common words can be added to the data set and recognised by the algorithm which improves performance iteratively.

7.6   Creating the data set

Every time the algorithm classifies a word image this image and its label is saved into what will be referred to as the "created data set". This is a data set that saves all labelled images found by the algorithm. The method by which the word is found is not considered. Words can be labelled by index matching, as described in section, by filling in spaces, as described in 7.5 or by close matches in the created data set built by previous pages, as described later in this section. This data set is an important result in itself since a data set can be used to classify words, even on images of pages without a matching transcript.

The notion "data set" is used to describe a set of data, a Python Dictionary, that the algorithm returns as its output. Each item in the set carries information about the image. Information such as the image itself, its position in the feature space, its position on the handwritten page in pixel coordinates but also, and of great importance, the label that the algorithm found. For each page the data returned from that page is considered an alignment since the label is connected to a position on the handwritten page. This is then added to the data set created from previous pages and constitutes the output denoted as the "created data set".

The created data set will grow from empty given that new words are found by index matching. This data set is used to find words that are not reoccurring on the page, but rather are very similar to an already labelled image in the created data set. If a word in this data set is very similar to a word on the page, before any index matching is done, the label is considered found. This is a more robust method since it is not affected by the misalignment between the transcript and the word images. These new aligned words, and words in gaps, as outlined in 7.5, will be added to the data set, which can be used to create better alignments on the next page provided to the algorithm.

The theory of the algorithm including the data set is simplified and outlined below.

Algorithm 1: The algorithm described

```
ds dst lim = maximum distance allowed in the data set feature space
ft dst lim = maximum distance allowed in the page feature space
word images = handwritten page as an array of word images
transcript = the transcript as an array of words
max gap size = maximum amount of words to be filled in in gap
last confirmed index = 0
for index in transcript do
    word image = word images[index]
    transcribed word = transcript[index]
    data set neighbour = neighbour to word image in data set
    ds dst = distance between word image and data set neighbour
    feature space neighbours = neighbours to word image in feature space
    if ds dst ≤ dsdstlim then
        save alignment;
        save to data set;
        if i - last confirmed index ≤ maxgapsize then
            fill gaps;
        end
        return
    else
        for feature space neighbour do
            neighbor index = index of feature space neighbour in word images
            ft dst = distance between word image and feature space neighbour
            if ft dst then
                if transcript[neighbor index] == transcript[index] then
                    save alignment;
                    save to data set;
                    if i - last confirmed index ≤ maxgapsize then
                        fill gaps;
                    else
                        return
                    end
                    return;
                else
            else
        end
    end
end
```

7.7   Edit distance

Edit distance is useful as the images found by the created data set can be considered labelled, the issue is the algorithm has no information about which of the words in the transcript this word actually represents. Words commonly found in the data, as can be seen in section 10.3 are for example a period. A period can reoccur in several places on a page. How can the algorithm know which instance this specific word image represents? A solution for this is to use edit distance. Edit distance is a measure that can be used to measure the difference between two sets of text, as outlined in section 4.6.

Edit distance is used as a measure to minimise, to find the optimal match between the transcript and all found words found both by index matching and by ground-truth. With the transcript and found words aligned each word image is aligned with the optimal word label in the transcript. By doing this the created data set is not only used to build the created data set further but also to align each page.

7.8   Parameters

In this section, the purpose and choices of parameters are described further.

7.8.1   Fill distance

As described in section 7.5 words in between two close confirmed words are considered confirmed if the number of word-images are the same as the amount of transcribed words in the gap. How small this gap must be is a parameter. For perfectly aligned test data this could in theory be as large as the page size. Although, as outlined in section 7.5, a gap size that too big carries risk of large miss-classification that will multiply through other pages. In testing this is set to 4 and visualised in blue. This is set to a low number to minimize the risk of miss-classification while still being able to find less common words.

7.8.2   Image neighbours

This measure is used to decide what images to consider when inspecting what word images could represent the same word. If only the closest Euclidean neighbour in the feature space is considered the amount of found words is lower than if the search is broadened to also look at the second and third neighbour. If the search instead is too wide the algorithm is more likely to by chance find matching words and incorrectly classify, which while creating a data set is not ideal. This is set to either 3 or 5 given the number of classified words compared to miss-classifications for that specific data, evaluated manually.

7.8.3   Word neighbours

The word neighbours to consider in the transcript suffer from the same issues as image neighbours in the feature space. These issues are that the percentage of found words is improved by adding words, however, the risk of miss-classification is also higher. The word neighbours considered in this book is the closest neighbour on either side of the word in the transcript, as well as the second closest. This results in 4 word-neighbours in total for each word. In testing, since the data is not misaligned, the word neighbour distance is set to 0 to decrease the risk of misalignment. In section 10.5 the measure is evaluated and discussed further for other values than 0.

7.8.4   Feature space max distance, image neighbours

To find images in the feature space representing the same word the closest words are deemed neighbours. If no images are similar the closest neighbours will still exist and are considered similar under false pretences. When comparing the neighbours a maximum Euclidean distance is enforced. This to make sure the considered neighbours are close in the feature space, not only the closest. This is set to a maximum distance of 20 for the IAM data set, evaluated for five different pages. The evaluation is done by comparing the distance in the feature space between images representing the same word to the images representing different words. Since evaluating if two word images represent the same word is done manually, this entire process is done manually. This parameter is not changed while testing on shorthand data.

7.8.5   Feature space max distance, created data set

While comparing words to the created data set what is considered a good match must be determined. Since there is no consideration for the place of the words in the transcript at this stage of the algorithm, the match must be certain based on the similarity of the images only. Since the algorithm uses the distance in the feature space as the similarity measure this is also used as the limit for the similarity of the images. This is set to a maximum distance of 6. Significantly closer than the measure described in 7.8.4. It is evaluated and set using the same method as in section 7.8.4, a manual comparison of images and feature space distances. This is evaluated for the pages shown in 10.3.

7.9   Evaluation methods

To assess the performance of the alignment in testing a few measures must be defined.

The main measure used to evaluate results is how many words of the page are given a correct label, this is referred to as a percentage of found words and is given by the total amount of word images the algorithm has given a label as a percentage of all words on a page. Words are found by either index matching, created data set comparison, or matching words and transcripts in small gaps.

Handwritten text recognition accuracy can be assessed in terms of the Word Error Rate (WER). It represents the number of edits required to convert results of the system into transcripts, as a percentage of the total number of transcribed words [20]. In the perfectly aligned texts seen in section 10.2, 10.3 and 10.4 this measure does not provide additional information, as all words not labelled or labelled incorrectly will represent the same information as WER. Instead, adapted measures are used to be able to evaluate each method separately and compare the results from these.

An important measure to be able to review results of index matching is to review the number of words found by index matching, landmark words, in comparison to the total amount of words that could in theory be found using this method. Because this method relies on the existence of several image representations of a reoccurring word on one page not all words can be matched in this way. The word images that are candidates to be matched in this way are representations of words that reoccur in the text, and where both word images are correctly transcribed. The percentage of landmark words found is referred to as the percentage of landmark words found given in relation to the total amount of landmark words that could be found which is the amount of reoccuring words.

The measures above are used together with the measure of miss-classification. Miss-classification is detrimental both to the alignment but also to the creation of the data set. A miss-labelled image in the created data set will far increase the risk of influencing future results negatively. A few correctly labelled words are often more useful than a larger data set partially miss labelled. Miss-labelling must therefore always be taken into account. The percentage of correctly labelled words is given as a percentage of labelled words.

8   Delimitations

In the following section delimitations of the work are explained.

8.1   Word segmentation

To be able to analyze words on a page word images must be extracted and separated from each other, this is commonly referred to as word segmentation. This is a well-studied subject and a science in itself. Word segmentation is not studied further in this book, the IAM data set used for English text is segmented by words, hence there is no need for segmentation algorithms on this data. For non-segmented data sets, word segmentation would have to be carried out beforehand. For the proof of concept created in this book the omission of efficient word segmentation is deemed acceptable.

To be able to test on shorthand data some manual word segmentation and labelling was carried out.

9   System structure

This section contains visualisations of the algorithm in the word segmentation, neighbour identifying initial steps as well as the transcript matching. The steps of word segmentation and neighbour identification in both the feature space and in the transcript are visualised in fig 1 3. In 1 4 the algorithm is resumed and the comparison between transcribed words as well as the filling of g aps. As an output the created data set is shown.

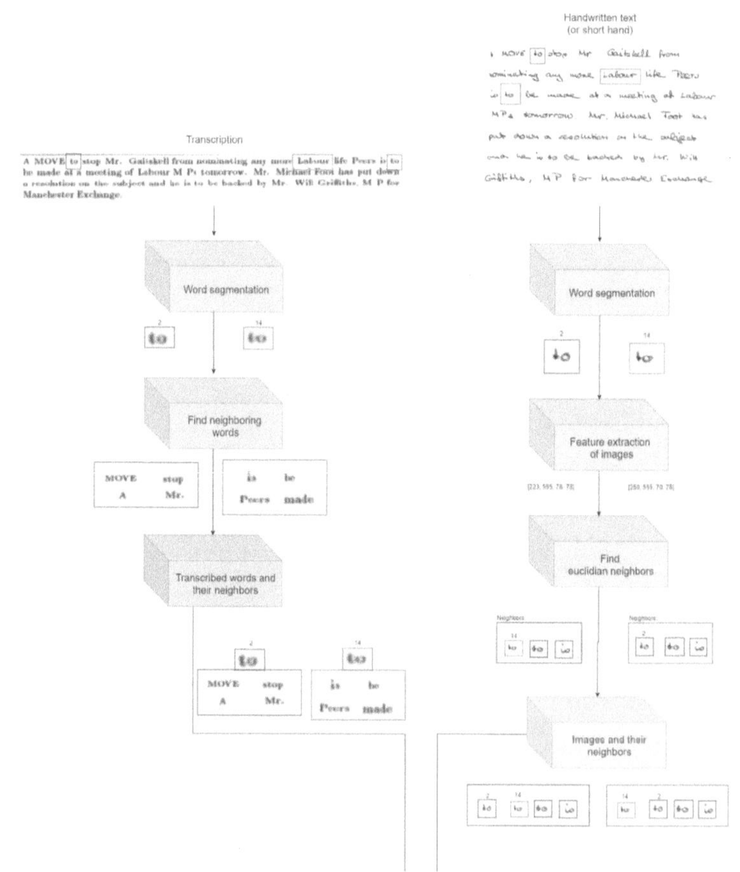

Figure 13 The system structure begins in this figure and shows two inputs, the transcript, on the left. And the handwritten text, on the right. Both inputs are word segmented. The segmented word images are each run through the CNN to receive a feature vector describing the image. These features are then used to give each word some neighbours with similar features. In the transcript each word is given a few adjacent words as neighbours. These words and their neighbours, defined in different ways, are then fed into the next part of the system, shown in 14.

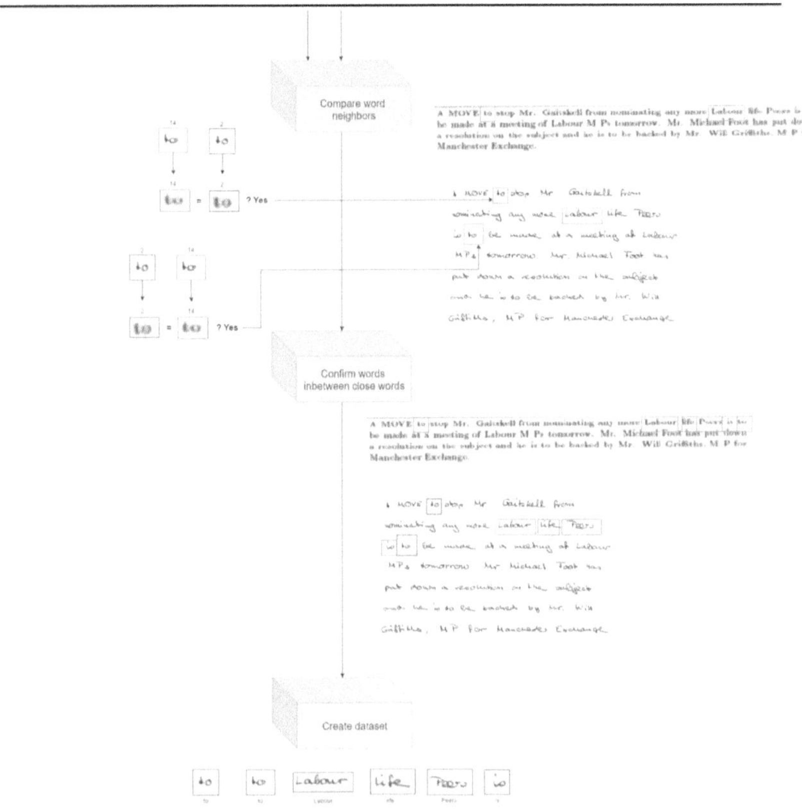

Figure 14 This figure follows figure 13 and shows the input of words in the transcript and adjacent words in the transcript. This as well as the similar words, defined as word images with similar feature vectors are fed into the system. This neighbour, in red, is used as an indicator for where the word would be transcribed. The word at this position in the transcript is equal to the word at the neighbors word at its position and therefore matched and saved. In the last step the spaces are filled in, shown in orange.

10   Results

In the following section, the results are accounted for and discussed. The parameters are explained thoroughly in section 7.8. The CNN is retrained between sections 10.2, 10.3 and 10.4. An important thing to note is that even though the CNN is retrained identical training data is used, no specialised data for shorthand is used while retraining for section 10.4.

For each page the algorithm is shown a page it returns a small data set of labelled images. This contains images and some alignment and label data for these. This is the result that constitutes the alignment. This entire page result data set is added to the created data set, which will make the data set grow.

In the next section,10.1 the accuracy of the CNN, as seen in training as a classifier, is shown for two cases of the number of epochs trained for.

In section 10.2 the results of the algorithm on one page at a time are presented. These results show the algorithm without taking the created data set into account, only index matching. This is shown for five different pages and visualised.

In section 10.3 10 pages are consecutively shown to the algorithm. Each page uses the created data set, accumulated from aligned images of all previous pages. This to make a more accurate alignment. Lastly, the results of a page aligned with the aid of a data set of 551 labelled word images are compared to the same page aligned with an empty data set, to illustrate the improvement the created data set contributes to. All references to the created data set in section 10.3 refer to the data set created and iteratively grown.

10.1   CNN and feature extraction

When the network is trained for 20 epochs it yields an accuracy of approximately 93% as seen in figure 15. As the improvements are small above 10 epochs the CNN is trained on 10 epochs in the final version, results for 10 epochs is shown in figure 16. In figure 17 some randomly chosen words are shown together with their neighbors in the feature space to visualise similarity.

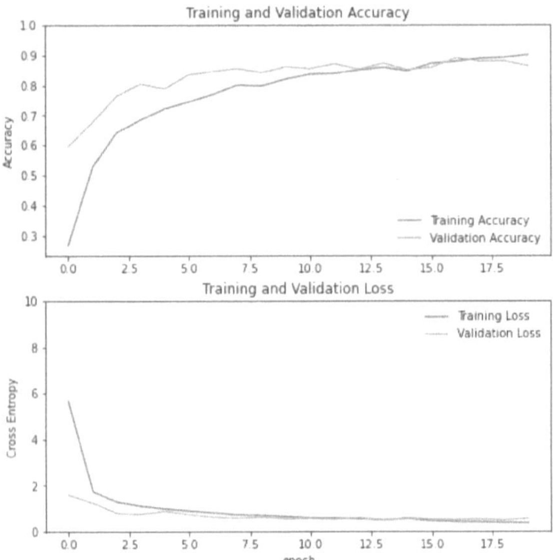

Figure 15 This graph shows the accuracy and loss over 20 epochs

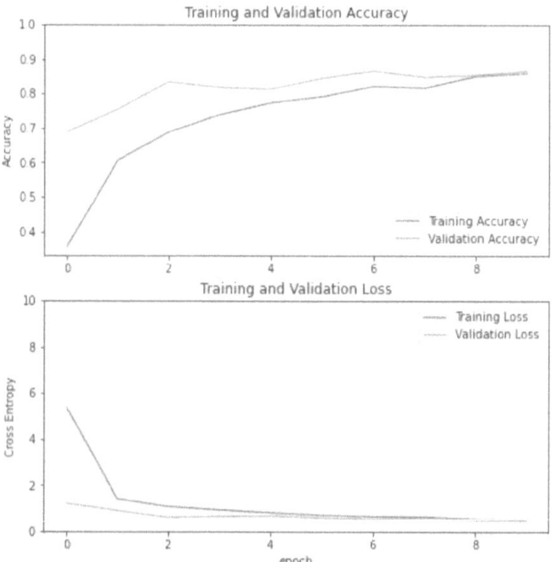

Figure 16 This graph shows the accuracy and loss over 10 epochs

Figure 17 Above the first 11 words of a randomly chosen page are shown as well as each words closest 3 neighbours in the feature space. The page is 026 from the IAM data set, which can be found in appendix A in figure 46. The neighbours are shown vertically where each column represents a word, the words on the top row are taken from the page in order. The following words in each column are the neighbours the CNN deems similar, in order of proximity.

10.2   Visualisation of results on one page

In this section, the algorithm on one page is tested. For each of the 5 pages shown in this section with a neighbour amount of 3, the results are visualised as coloured squares on the page each enclosing a correctly labelled word. Green squares correspond to words that have been found by finding neighbours in the feature space and matching neighbours to their corresponding place in the transcript. This is described in detail in section 10.3 and is referred to as index matching in this book. The words found by this method are referred to as landmark words. Blue squares are words that are found by matching the number of words in the image and transcript between two landmark words. All words found, regardless of by which method, are saved to the created data set.

All pages in their original form can be found in appendix A.

Page name	003	007	011	020	026
Landmark words	26	20	18	24	22
Reouccuring words	33	23	24	25	24
Percentage landmark words	79%	87%	75%	96%	92%
Filled words	24	21	21	20	31
Found words total	57	48	47	48	46
Total words	81	69	68	68	77
Percentage found	70%	70%	69%	71%	60%
Accuracy of labeled words	100%	100%	100%	100%	100%

Figure 18 Results for 5 pages shown to the algorithm with an empty data set for all pages. This results in an average percentage of found words of 72% of the entire page and the percentage of found landmark words is an average of 86%.

Sentence Database   A01-003

Though they may gather some Left-wing support, a large majority of Labour M Ps
are likely to turn down the Foot-Griffiths resolution. Mr. Foot's line will be that as
Labour M Ps opposed the Government Bill which brought life peers into existence,
they should not now put forward nominees. He believes that the House of Lords
should be abolished and that Labour should not take any steps which would appear
to "prop up" an out-dated institution.

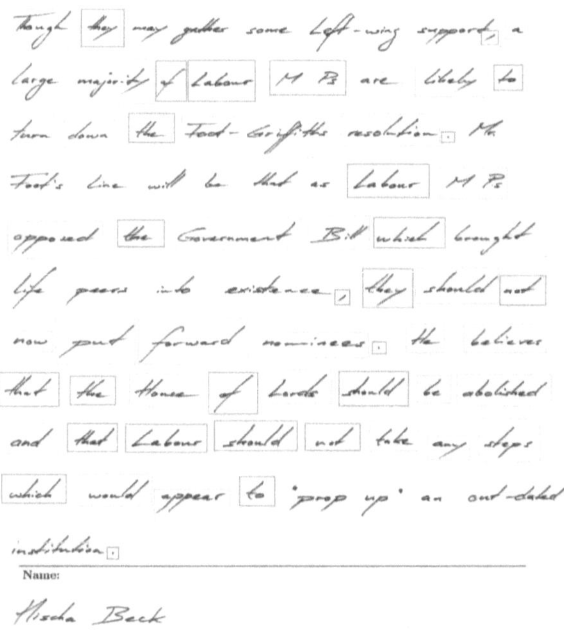

Name:

Figure 19 This image shows a page, A01-003, from the IAM data set which has been
shown to the algorithm on an empty data set. The percentage of found words on the page
is 70%. To visualise how the neighbours in the feature space are found these neighbours
for the landmark words are shown in figure 24.

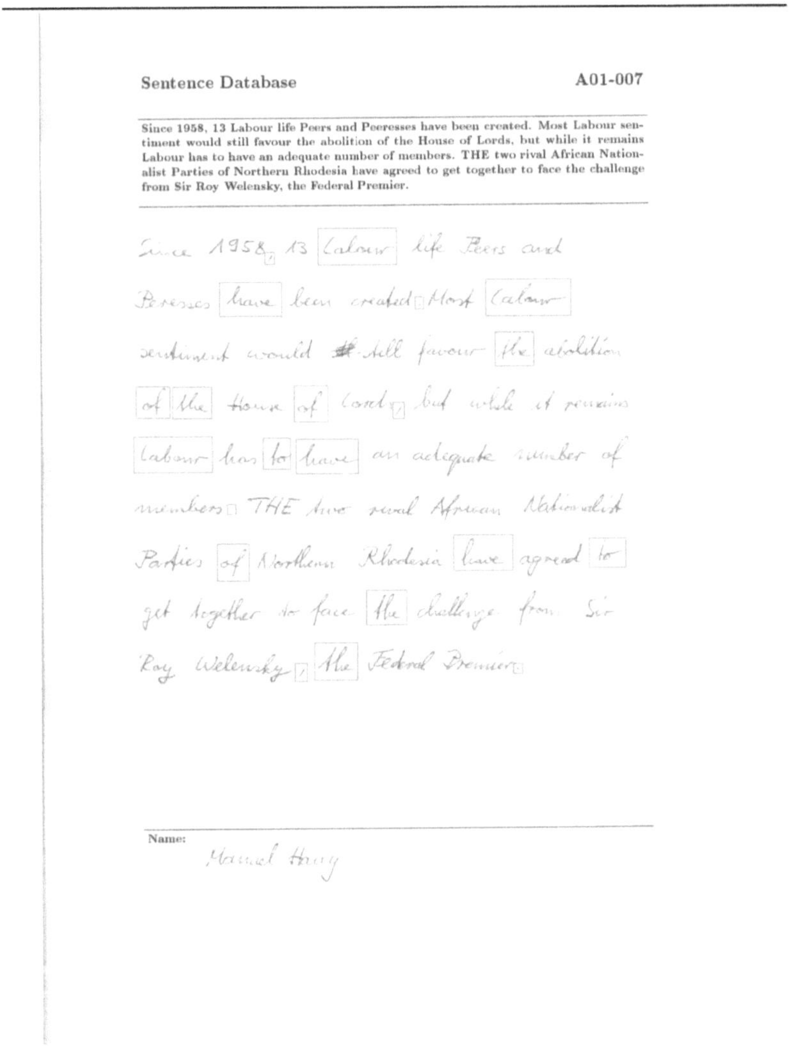

Sentence Database   A01-007

Since 1958, 13 Labour life Peers and Peeresses have been created. Most Labour sentiment would still favour the abolition of the House of Lords, but while it remains Labour has to have an adequate number of members. THE two rival African Nationalist Parties of Northern Rhodesia have agreed to get together to face the challenge from Sir Roy Welensky, the Federal Premier.

Since 1958, 13 Labour life Peers and Peeresses have been created. Most Labour sentiment would still favour the abolition of the House of Lords, but while it remains Labour has to have an adequate number of members. THE two rival African Nationalist Parties of Northern Rhodesia have agreed to get together to face the challenge from Sir Roy Welensky, the Federal Premier.

Name: Manuel Hug

Figure 20 This image shows a page, A01-007, from the IAM data set which has been shown to the algorithm on an empty data set. The percentage of all found words on the page is 70%.

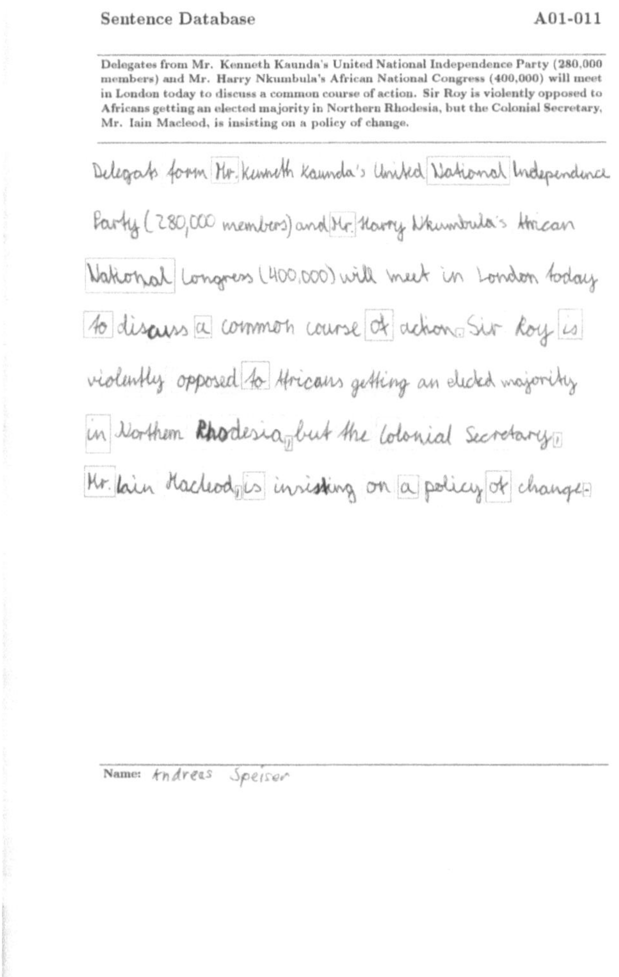

Sentence Database   A01-011

Delegates from Mr. Kenneth Kaunda's United National Independence Party (280,000 members) and Mr. Harry Nkumbula's African National Congress (400,000) will meet in London today to discuss a common course of action. Sir Roy is violently opposed to Africans getting an elected majority in Northern Rhodesia, but the Colonial Secretary, Mr. Iain Macleod, is insisting on a policy of change.

Delegats form Mr. Kenneth Kaunda's United National Independence Party (280,000 members) and Mr. Harry Nkumbula's African National Congress (400,000) will meet in London today to discuss a common course of action. Sir Roy is violently opposed to Africans getting an elected majority in Northern Rhodesia, but the Colonial Secretary, Mr. Iain Macleod, is insisting on a policy of change.

Name: Andreas Speiser

Figure 21 This image shows a page, A01-011, from the IAM data set which has been shown to the algorithm on an empty data set. The percentage of all found words on the page is 69%.

Sentence Database   A01-020

Mr. Macleod went on with the conference at Lancaster House despite the crisis
which had blown up. He has now revealed his full plans to the Africans and Liberals
attending. These plans do not give the Africans the overall majority they are seeking.
African delegates are studying them today. The conference will meet to discuss the
function of a proposed House of Chiefs.

Mr. MacLeod went on with the conference at
Lancaster House despite the crisis which had
blown up. He has now revealed his full plans
to the africans and Liberals attending. These
plans do not give the Africans the overall
majority they are seeking. African delegates
are studying them today. The conference
will meet to discuss the function of a
proposed House of Chiefs.

Name:
Guido Kaufmann

Figure 22 This image shows a page, A01-020, from the IAM data set which has been shown to the algorithm on an empty data set. The percentage of all found words on the page is 71%.

Sentence Database   A01-026

MR. IAIN MACLEOD, the Colonial Secretary, denied in the Commons last night that
there have been secret negotiations on Northern Rhodesia's future. The Northern
Rhodesia conference in London has been boycotted by the two main settlers' parties
- the United Federal Party and the Dominion Party. But representatives of Sir Roy
Welensky, Prime Minister of the Central African Federation, went to Chequers at the
week-end for talks with Mr. Macmillan.

MR. IAIN MACLEOD, the Colonial Secretary, denied
in the Commons last night that there have been
secret negotiations on Northern Rhodesia's future.
The Northern Rhodesia conference in London has
been boycotted by the two main settlers' parties -
the United Federal Party and the Dominion Party.
But representatives of Sir Roy Welensky, Prime
Minister of the Central African Federation, went
to Chequers at the week-end for talks with
Mr. Macmillan.

Name:
Guido Kaufmann

Figure 23 This image shows a page, A01-026, from the IAM data set which has been shown to the algorithm on an empty data set. The percentage of all found words on the page is 60%.

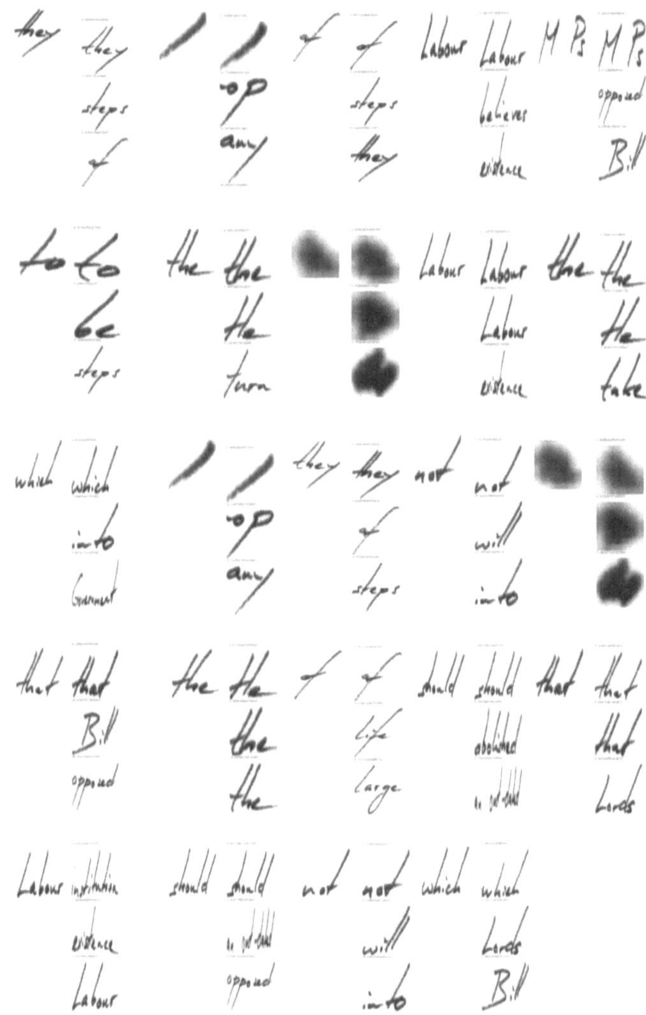

Figure 24 This image shows the feature space neighbours for the words that act as landmark words in the page shown in figure 19.

10.3   Improvements with data set creation

In this section the results of the algorithm is shown when passed 11 pages from the IAM data set and using iterative expansion of created data set with correctly classified images. This to create better alignments and further additions to this created data set. This is described as the created data set, which will save each labelled word for subsequent pages to refer to. This is considered in itself an important result be be able to analyse future works and the size and growth of this data set is outlined in this section. Results are also visualised for a few pages. All visualisations follow the same pattern, words enclosed in squares are correctly labelled, the colour of the square described the method through which it was labelled. Green represents landmark words, purple represents words found in the created data set and blue are words that are filled in spaces between confirmed words. Images of each page in this section can be found in the appendix A.

In figure 25 the results of this section are given. The algorithm is run on 10 pages with a neighbour distance of 5. For each page the data set is iteratively grown. The size of the data set reaches 495 at page 9, and uses this to create better alignments. The results of the last page is visualized in 26 using coloured boxes to reference words found by different methods. Lastly a page is shown the resulting data set of 551 images is compared to the same page without the data set, the results are shown in 27. In this result the pages are shown with a higher neighbour distance of 10. The labels were manually inspected for miss-classification.

Page	000u	003u	007u	011u	020u	026u	030u	043u	049u	053u
Total classified words on page, including filled	24	59	50	63	52	45	70	36	62	34
Total words on page	52	80	68	68	68	77	85	68	75	67
Total percentage found, all methods	46%	74%	74%	93%	76%	58%	82%	53%	83%	51%
Classified landmark words	14	23	16	20	19	12	20	13	19	10
Possible landmark words	16	32	23	24	25	24	34	20	28	24
Percentage of landmark words found	88%	72%	70%	83%	76%	50%	59%	65%	68%	42%
Words found by created data set	0	2	4	3	4	5	9	5	6	6
Data set percetage of entire page	0%	3%	6%	4%	6%	6%	11%	7%	8%	9%
Label accuracy	100%	99%	100%	100%	100%	100%	100%	100%	100%	100%
Total created data set size	0	24	68	133	196	293	363	399	461	495

Figure 25 In this image the results are shown when providing the algorithm 10 pages using a data set neighbour distance of 5. The first page shown in this section is A01-000u from the IAM data set, the rest of the images are then shown in order from left to right in the table. Each of the images accounted for can be found in its original state in appendix A. For each page shown the created data set grows larger as can be seen in bottom row of the table. The percentage of total words classified of all words on that page is shown in row 3 "percentage found" and is the quota of classified words on page and total words on page (row 1 and 2). Similarly the percentage of words in the page that are classified from the created data set is shown in row 'Data set percentage of entire page', based on row 2 and 7. The amount of landmark words found is shown on row "Percentage of landmark words found". The last important measure is the accuracy of found labels, which is shown in "label accuracy".

Figure 26 The 053u page without the data set of 461 images using a max neighbour distance of 5. The colored squares represent correctly labelled words found by different methods. Green represents landmark words, correctly labelled words by index matching. Purple boxes represent words found by the created data set. Blue represents words that are filled in gaps. This figure is a visualisation of the data shown in the last column of the table shown in figure 25.

Page	058u	058u without data set
Total classified words on page, including filled	56	44
Total words on page	67	67
Total percentage found, all methods	84%	66%
Classified landmark words	17	19
Possible landmark words	24	24
Percentage of landmark words found	71%	79%
Words found by created data set	17	0
Data set percetage of entire page	25%	0%
Label accuracy	100%	100%
Total created data set size	551	0

Figure 27 This figure shows detailed results of running the page A01-058 u with a neighbour distance of 10 and a data set of 551 images. This data set is created by the 10 pages referenced in figure 25 and the rows represent the same values. Visualisation of these pages are shown in figure 28 and 29.

Figure 28 This page shows the results of the algorithm on the IAM page A01-058u using a created data set of 551 labels. The colored squares represent correctly labelled words found by different methods. Green represents landmark words, labelled words by index matching. Purple boxes represent words found by the created data set. Blue represents words that are filled in gaps.

Figure 29 This page shows the results of the algorithm on the IAM page A01-058u using a created data set that is set to empty before running the algorithm. The colored squares represent correctly labelled words found by different methods. Green represents landmark words, labelled words by index matching. Purple boxes represent words found by the created data set, since no created data set is used no purple boxes are shown. Blue represents words that are filled in gaps.

10.4   Shorthand results

In this section the algorithm is tested on some shorthand data taken from two sources. The following section shows a few rows of shorthand from a Melin shorthand text book [22]. The page has been pre-processed and has been manually transcribed by the author of this book. The neighbours of the landmark words in the feature space are shown in figure 3 2. In section 1 0.4.2 a shorthand page from the Wikipedia page [3] is used for testing.

10.4.1   Outtake from textbook on Melin shorthand

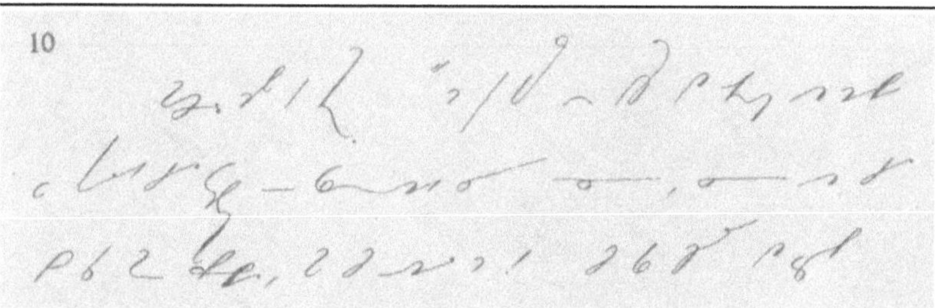

Figure 30 This figure shows a 41 shorthand words written in Melin shorthand before any pre-processing

The author of this book has transcribed the words on this page into:

"Majorn Täng en stunder. 'Det är väl inte endast ett anbud att tacka för svarade han stöddigt och fortsatte, si oså, så att han skulle se då senare, men jag antar det! Jag vill höra ett utrop"

10

Figure 31 This figure shows a 41 shorthand words written in Melin shorthand pre-processed.

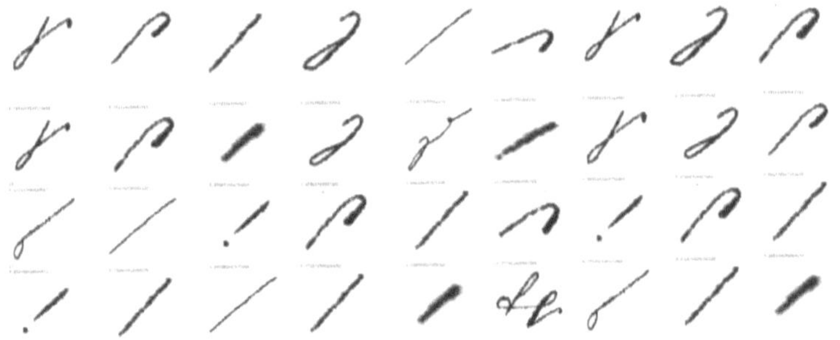

Figure 32 This image shows the CNN's feature extraction and how well the distancing in the feature space functions for shorthand. Similarly to in figure 17 the words and their neighbours are shown as columns. Important to keep in minds is the fact that this figure shows the neighbours that go on to create a match and correspond to 23% of the total words on the page tested.

10

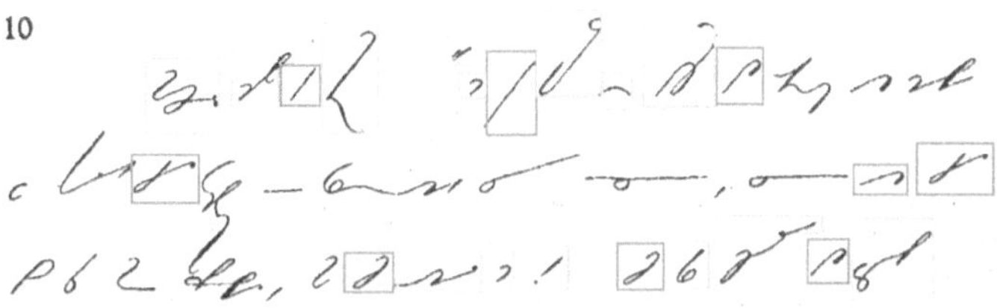

Figure 33 This figure shows the results of the algorithm on the shorthand data using a created data set that is set to empty before running the algorithm. The colored squares represent correctly labelled words found by different methods. Green represents landmark words, labelled words by index matching. Blue represents words that are filled in gaps.

10.4.2   Melin shorthand Wikipedia page

The transcription given by [3] the Wikipedia page is written below.

"Korthet och snabbskrifvenhet äro onekligen viktiga egenskaper hos stenografien, men af fullt ut lika stor betydelse är tillförlitligheten och tydligheten, och där den saknas, har man intet egentligt gagn för det praktiska lifvet af kunskapen i stenografi. Det system, som visar sig bäst motsvara anspråken på tydlighet, skall därför i längden komma att stå som segrare i striden mellan de olika metoderna."

This text, if regarding periods and commas as words as is done in previous testing, is 68 words long. The amount of word images shown below is instead 62 words. The misalignment of 6 words violates assumption 1 from section 3, but can be easily adjusted by removing periods and commas, which are not used in this authors writing. Instead of dots representing the end of a sentence, dots are an abbreviation of the word "det" (the word "it" in English). Shorthand does not utilize uppercase letters, so transforming all letters into lowercase will facilitate a better alignment. By these simple measures, removing periods and commas and transforming all letters to lowercase, the result of the algorithm is shown in figure 34, with the transformed transcript below.

"korthet och snabbskrifvenhet äro onekligen viktiga egenskaper hos stenografien men af fullt ut lika stor betydelse är tillförlitligheten och tydligheten och där den saknas har man intet egentligt gagn för det praktiska lifvet af kunskapen i stenografi det system som visar sig bäst motsvara anspråken på tydlighet skall därför i längden komma att stå som

segrare i striden mellan de olika metoderna"

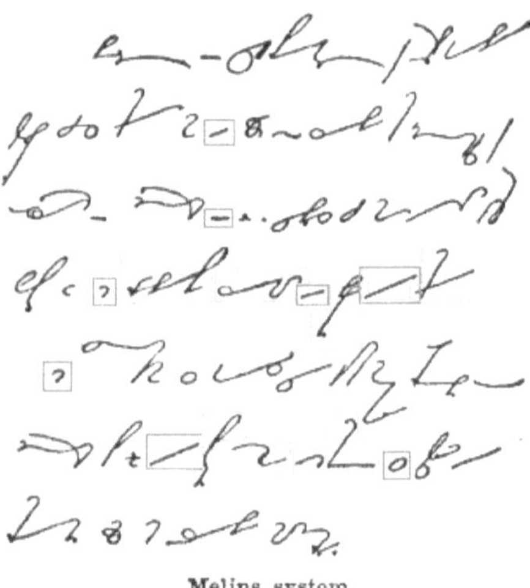

Figure 34 An example of the result of the algorithm run on a page of shorthand, with the transcript transformed by removing periods and commas, and only using lowercase letters. The green squares represent correctly labelled words using index matching. blue squares represent filled in words.

Another specific issue with this transcript and shorthand page is the usage of the word "äro", this word is an old plural form of the word "är". "äro" and "är" have the same shorthand representation, this since the abbreviation for both words is the same. This violates assumption 2 from section 3 outlining the visual representations of words. By changing the word "äro" to "är" in the transcript, a better alignment can be found. The transcript after this transformation is shown below, and the result after this transformation is shown in figure 35.

"korthet och snabbskrifvenhet är onekligen viktiga egenskaper hos stenografien men af fullt ut lika stor betydelse är tillförlitligheten och tydligheten och där den saknas har man intet egentligt gagn för det praktiska lifvet af kunskapen i stenografi det system som visar sig bäst motsvara anspråken på tydlighet skall därför i längden komma att stå som segrare i striden mellan de olika metoderna"

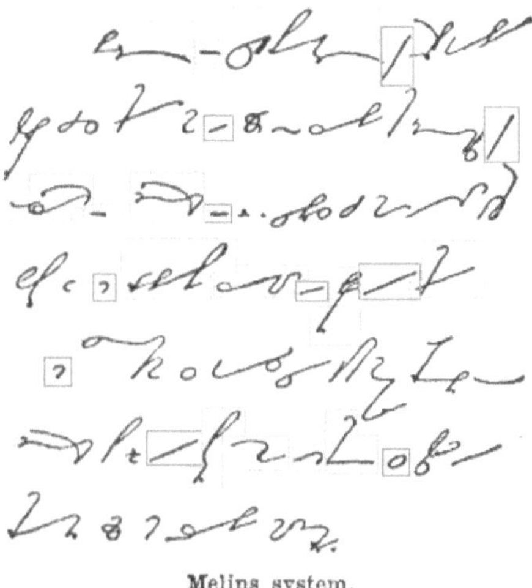

Figure 35 An example of the result of the algorithm run on a page of shorthand, with the transcript transformed by removing periods and commas, only using lowercase letters and translating the word "äro" into "är". The green squares represent correctly labelled words using index matching. blue squares represent filled in words.

10.5 Misalignment

This section is used to verify results on misaligned data using no data set. This has been tested to be able to assess the results on pages that are not perfectly aligned. The pages are misaligned by adding an additional word in the transcript at the very first position, this results in all following words being misaligned. There are two important parts to keep in mind while evaluating these results. One is all classified words, how well the algorithm finds words at all on these misaligned pages. One other measure is more important to assess the results on misaligned pages. This measure is the miss-classification of words. A data set where miss-classified images are common becomes less valuable as training or analysis data than data that is well classified. Some values where the balance between these two measures on one page is shown in figure 36. No created data set was used in this testing.

Max distance	20	20	10	10
Neighbors	5	3	5	3
Correctly classfified words	3	3	0	0
Miss-classified words	5	1	0	0

Figure 36 This table shows the results for misaligned text of the IAM page A01-003u, offset by 1, taking into account two amounts of neighbours and two maximum neighbour distances. No created data set is used in this testing. The combination of max distance in the feature space and the amount of neighbours considered are inspected to evaluate the risk of miss-classification.

11   Discussion

In this section, the results are discussed and conclusions are drawn about the efficiency of the algorithm on some data.

11.1   CNN classification accuracy

In this section, the result of the CNN in training is discussed.

As seen in figure 15 when trained for 20 epochs yields an accuracy of 93%. As is also illustrated by this graph the accuracy above 10 epochs did not improve enough to warrant continued training. Continued training could result in over-fitting, as described in section 4.1. In subsequent testing, CNN's trained for 10 epochs were used. For 10 epochs the accuracy reaches approximately 85% implying the network has learnt the shape of word images while training in classification and is in most cases correct. Considering selecting a class randomly statistically would result in 5% correct classifications for 20 classes. This proves that the CNN has learnt the shape of the words and can separate them. As can be seen in the results in the sections 10.2, 10.3 and 10.4. Since this project serves as a proof of concept for the alignment of handwritten text images with transcripts without the need for labelled training data the accuracy of the CNN is deemed adequate. This claim is supported by figure 17 where a randomly chosen page is used to assess neighbours in the feature space. On this randomly chosen page, A01-026, the 11 first words are chosen, to be able to manually verify the similarity of neighbours in the feature space. As can be seen, common words are grouped, the word "the" is close to three other instances of the word in the feature space. Commas group to other commas, and the word "in" is deemed the closest neighbour to the only other instance of "in" in the text. Not all words can neighbour another instance of the same word, since many only occur once. This is the case for all words not mentioned but shown in the figure. Note "Mr." and "MR." are not deemed the same word in the tests on English text. This can be manually verified on the page AO1-026 shown in appendix A in figure 46.

Since the CNN in this case is trained on the same type of data, as is used in the alignment, it is natural that it is optimised for the shape of these words and would yield worse results on other types of data. The expectation is that even if the CNN has not learnt to distinguish the specific shapes in the data the CNN can do some type of distinction between types of words. Since the algorithm is based on a nearest-neighbour-principle the feature extraction does not have to be perfect since the assumption is that similar words will still be closer in the feature space than words that are not similar. This must not be true for all types of data. One important thing to consider is that the closeness of the words in the feature space determines the parameters that set the limit for what is determined a match. These parameters are outlined in section 7.8.4 and 7.8.5, and these must be adjusted to each case to avoid mislabeling the data.

As can be seen in section 10.4 the assumption that the feature extraction will give similar shorthand words similar features in the same way it does for English words, without retraining of the CNN, appears to be correct. This is shown in figure 32 where the landmark word neighbours have been visualised with images. It can distinguish between different shorthand words, and creates an alignment of 22% of landmark words resulting in 56% after filling gaps. This is equivalent to a labelled data set of 23 words after a single page of 41 words. The algorithm overlooks some possibilities for landmark words. Such as commas, two commas occur in the text, but the commas are not neighbours in the feature space created so they are not classified. Only one of the two words representing the Swedish word "är" is classified. They occur at position 13 and 25 and the first instance of the word is a close neighbour to the second instance of the word. The second instance of the word has other closer neighbours, none of which was the other occurrence of the word. This results in only one instance of the word being classified.

11.2   Results of index matching

In section 10.2 the results of using index matching and filling the gaps between landmark words is shown for several pages. No new data set is built linking these pages. The average result over the five pages is 68% aligned words, this shows that the algorithm is functional on several different pages of handwritten English text, with a consistent result for the language tested. Note that each of these pages contains different text and are written by different authors, showing the functionality of the concept on the IAM data set.

11.3   Line data and segmentation robustness

One of the assumptions outlined in section 3 is that "The transcript is fairly similar to the page layout, with only occasional added or dropped words.". This assumption is an important pillar the algorithm lies on. A more robust algorithm is favourable, if an entire line is added or removed ideally the algorithm can take that into account. While using real-life word segmentation algorithms the situation where entire lines are missed is not uncommon and therefore important to take into account in the case where word segmentation is not done manually. This could be done by taking into account the words position in the transcript in a more detailed way. This is described further in 13.

11.4   The created data set

The data set created by the algorithm is an important part of the algorithm as this is what in practice makes it grow more intelligent and robust as it is shown more data. An alignment of 66%, as is shown in figure 27 on each page will still slowly grow a data set to be considered a result. Disregarding the information collected in the created data set is a waste of the data at hand. Instead, the images collected in the created data set are kept in a new instance of the same feature space, using the same features they were designated when they were first classified. Each time a new word is found the algorithm first examines the created data set feature space and finds the closest Euclidean neighbour. One important thing to note is since this is not a comparison between two similar words on the page the distance in the feature space must be close. As outlined in 7.8 a maximum limit for the distance in the created data set feature space must be set to make sure only extremely similar words will classify as two images representing the same word. As the created data set grows larger the probability of any word on a page existing in the data set feature space grows, and therefore the probability of being able to classify images without taking index into account grows. This is important since the algorithm is not too robust to misalignment of the data, if words are added or removed the percentage found is decreased. This is discussed further in section 10.5. Note that the tests are done on perfectly aligned test data. This helps the algorithm in the first steps while building the data set but becomes less important as more words are found as matches in the created data set feature space as opposed to index matching over the page.

The importance of using the created data set is illustrated in section 10.3, summarized in figure 25. On the first page shown to the algorithm, 000u, no data set has yet been built, and the 14 landmark words are found by index matching. A total of 24 words, including images in filled gaps, are saved as labelled images in the created data set and is used to help in classifying the next page, 003u. This page reaches a percentage of found words of 72% where 2 of the words are classified by the created data set as opposed to index matching. Both of these two are periods. A period is as can be seen in previous results fairly easy for the algorithm to recognise due to the characters particular shape. It is therefore fairly likely that the algorithm would have classified the periods without the help of the created data set.

What is important to keep in mind is that the created data set matching is not sensitive to misalignment of the data which the initial index matching technique is not. To analyse the third page, 007u, the data set found in 003u and 000u are combined into 68 labelled images, of which 4 are then used to classify the words of 007u, as opposed to by index matching. The total percentage of found words is identical to the previous page but the amount of words classified from the created data set is a larger percentage of the words found. This trend continues, the percentage of words found by the created data set increases when the data set grows, without any direct correlation with the overall percentage of found words that can be seen in test data.

What is interesting is showing the algorithm at the 10th page, A01-058u. Results from this page is shown in 27. where 25% of the found words are found through the created data set and the percentage of words found is 84%. On this page, the importance of the created data set is shown by running the algorithm on the same page and parameters but with an empty data set. The percentage of found words is decreased by 18% which can be viewed as proof that a data set will improve results. From that one can assume that increasing the size of the created data set will increase the percentage of found words. Larger scale tests would be needed to confirm this idea.

One key to data set classification is that the texts on each page must be fairly similar. This follows the fourth assumption made in section 3 defining that the text must be fairly uniform. The algorithm should then be able to align by recurring words, such as names or places with increasing accuracy.

One issue with aligning by data set is that this classification by data set is done on a word-image basis. The algorithm can find the label of an image using the created data set, but it cannot know which of the words in the transcript this word actually represents as outlined in 4.6. This is where edit distance can be utilised, to align the found labels to the transcript in the most probable way.

A way to utilise the created data set is to manually create an artificial data set before the first page is shown. This to be able to align some words using the data set, even before the algorithm adds any words. This data set could contain common words and their labels, to facilitate a better alignment. For shorthand official abbreviations of words could be added to a data set, as these tend to be common words. Using this technique alignment could be done more effectively and does not require much pre-processing.

11.5 Shorthand

In section 10.4 the algorithm is tested on two shorthand texts. This to investigate if the assumptions made in section 3 also hold for shorthand texts. The text in section 10.4.1 was transcribed manually and segmented, word by word, by the author of this book. This rendered a transcript with no misalignment.

This contrasts to section 10.4.2 where the transcript is given by the article. The author of the text, Melin himself, uses a few abbreviations and does not use punctuation. The transcript does use punctuation and that results in a misalignment of 6 words. To combat this punctuation is removed from the transcript, as this is considered a simple and consistent way to improve algorithm performance. Since shorthand does not distinguish uppercase letters from lowercase letters, the transcript has been transformed into entirely lowercase. These two forms of pre-processing of the transcript could be consistently applied over all transcripts shown to the algorithm, given that the writing style is consistent. This means all transcripts of shorthand texts written by Olof Melin could be processed in this way which is why the transformation of the transcript is deemed acceptable. These transformations result in 26% of the words on the page being correctly labelled.

A similar transformation that can be done to improve performance is changing the word "äro" into "är" in the transcript. This since both of these variations of the same word, have the same shorthand representation. This is due to an old plural form of the word. Carrying out this transformation in the transcript results in the alignment shown in figure 35, where 39% of the words on the page are correctly labelled. This transformation is carried out with caution as knowledge of the language and the transcript is needed to be able to safely make these transformations of the transcript.

The results shown in section 10.4 show that shorthand text fulfills the assumptions the algorithm lies on, after some processing of the transcripts. The algorithm produces an alignment of words from the very first page. Something that must be considered is pre-processing of the transcript, as well as the page. Following some simple rules, the transcript can be transformed into a text that can be more accurately aligned. The image can be processed into a high contrast image, where the words are clear and distinguished from the background.

11.6 Misalignment

In section 10.5 some results are shown for a misaligned text. These results show that by lowering the max distance of the neighbours in the feature space no words are classified, resulting in a classification percentage of 0%. This can be considered a bad result, but what is important to consider is that a miss-classification can contribute to a data set that is more difficult to use for training and analysis. In addition to a data set of worse quality is a bad result in itself, this data set is then used for subsequent pages to create alignments. Introducing images with incorrect labels will run the risk of affecting future results negatively. The assumption made is based on figure 36 and is that for misaligned pages the choice is between two bad results. Either a few correctly labelled images and a few miss-labelled images, or no images labelled if no good matches can be found. This is important, only well-classified images should be returned, regardless of how few words this results in being classified.

Allowing the misaligned pages to return worse alignment percentage results is an issue that must be addressed in some way. This is done by using the created data set to align word based on image similarity only, without regarding index. This is described in section 11.4. By providing the algorithm pages with both aligned and misaligned data some words will be stored in the data set and hence make future data less sensitive to misalignment. Another approach to combat this is to manually create some data set of common words before the algorithm is run, to simulate showing the algorithm aligned data it can classify by index matching.

12   Conclusion

The algorithm created through this book can be considered a proof of concept for the alignment of images of handwritten pages with corresponding transcripts. This is shown for English handwritten text and tested for a small amount of shorthand data and is built on four assumptions about the handwritten page and the transcript.

It yields a result of 68% correctly labelled words on one page of data, based on the similarity of word images and the position of the words on the page. The similarity of word images is determined by a CNN that has been trained as a classifier on English handwritten data and is used for feature extraction on each word image.

This algorithm is also tested on a small amount of shorthand data, to evaluate if the assumption that the CNN trained on a data set of historical English texts can also determine the visual similarity of words in a different language. The data tested is small but the results are promising. Some pre-processing on the transcripts was needed, but the algorithm functions as intended.

The area where the algorithm shows especially useful is related to but separate from word wise alignment and is data set creation. By using the results from the algorithm as a data set results can be improved as the algorithm is shown more pages. It is also in itself an important result as it is a labelled data set. Labelled data sets can be used for a variety of different analysis techniques.

13   Future work

The algorithm in its current state has several factors that could be improved.

Currently, the algorithm assesses the nearest neighbour in the feature space of the created data set to set a label. A maximum distance limit is set to prevent miss-classification. A different approach that might perform better is using some clustering algorithm on the data in the created data set each time it is updated. A new word could then be placed in the feature space and if they fit in an already defined cluster this can be considered a better match. If these clusters are created in such a way that they each correspond to a label the amount of found words might be higher, as it becomes less dependant on Euclidean distance. Using a clustering method occasional miss-classifications become less influential, as one wrong label is less likely to miss-classify future labels.

Transfer learning is the act of using a trained network on a certain type of data and then "continuing" training on specified data. When the created data set is large enough transfer learning can be used to be able to take advantage of the large amount of word data it is originally trained on as well as the data of the specific language the algorithm is to be used on. A simpler way to utilise the created data set is to simply run the same pages through the algorithm again after building a robust data set. This to give each page a chance to learn from future pages, and not only the converse.

Using data about what line each word resides on the algorithm could take into account the case where no matches are found on the current line, but match on the next, and if lines are overlooked in segmentation these could be "skipped" in the transcript. This is not currently implemented but would make the solution more robust for skipped or added lines.

In its current state the CNN only accepts square 225×225 images. If the images did not have to be re-scaled some more information about the word might be able to be used. Redesigning the CNN to accept different image sizes might result in better alignments and should be investigated.

Testing on larger data sets would be needed to confirm the conclusions drawn for smaller data, as has been done in this book. Testing on larger sets of shorthand data, but also testing on other types of data in other languages. The conclusion drawn for English historic text and a small amount of shorthand data seem to suggest the theory holds.

References

[1] "Astrid lindgrens arkiv på kungliga biblioteket," https://www.astridlindgren.com/
sv/astrid-lindgren/arvet-efter-astrid-lindgren/astrid-lindgrens-arkiv, accessed:
2021-05-05.

[2] "Handwriting recognition using cnn," https://tejasreddy9.github.io/handwriting_
cnn/, accessed: 2010-04-21.

[3] "Melin short hand," https://en.wikipedia.org/wiki/Melin_Shorthand, accessed:
2021-05-15.

[4] "Om astrid lindgren," https://www.astridlindgrensallskapet.se/om-astrid-
lindgren/, accessed: 2021-05-05.

[5] "Om astrid lindgren-koden," https://www.barnboksinstitutet.se/forskning/astrid-
lindgren-koden/, accessed: 2021-05-05.

[6] "Stenografi - ett eget rövarspråk," https://www.astridlindgren.com, accessed:
2021-05-07.

[7] "Towards dropout training for convolutional neural networks," *Neural Networks*,
vol. 71, pp. 1–10, 2015.

[8] "Text alignment in early printed books combining deep learning and dynamic pro-
gramming," *Pattern Recognition Letters*, vol. 133, pp. 109–115, 2020.

[9] O. Campesato, *Artificial intelligence, machine learning, and deep learning.*
Boston, Massachusetts;New Delhi;Dulles, Virginia;: Mercury Learning and Information, 2020.

[10] O. Campesato, *Artificial intelligence, machine learning, and deep learning.*
Boston, Massachusetts;New Delhi;Dulles, Virginia;: Mercury Learning and Information, 2020.

[11] T. H. Cormen, C. E. Leiserson, R. L. Rivest, C. Stein, and I. Books24x7, *Introduction to Algorithms, Third Edition*, 3rd ed. Cambridge: MIT Press, 2009.

[12] H. El-Amir, M. Hamdy, and S. O. service), *Deep Learning Pipeline: Building a Deep Learning Model with TensorFlow*, 1st ed. Berkeley, CA: Apress,
2020;2019;.

[13] I. Goodfellow, Y. Bengio, and A. Courville, *Deep Learning.* MIT Press, 2016,
http://www.deeplearningbook.org.

[14] M. Kulkarni, S. S. Karande, and S. Lodha, "Unsupervised word clustering using deep features," in *2016 12th IAPR Workshop on Document Analysis Systems (DAS)*, 2016.

[15] U.-V. Marti and H. Bunke, "The iam-database: An english sentence database for offline handwriting recognition," *International Journal on Document Analysis and Recognition*, vol. 5, pp. 39–46, 11 2002.

[16] O. W. Melin, *Stenografiens Historia, Andra delen.* Stockholm A.B Nordiska Bokhandeln, 1929.

[17] U. Michelucci and S. O. service), *Applied Deep Learning: A Case-Based Approach to Understanding Deep Neural Networks.* Berkeley, CA: Apress, 2018.

[18] U. Michelucci and S. O. service), *Advanced Applied Deep Learning: Convolutional Neural Networks and Object Detection*, 1st ed. Berkeley, CA: Apress, 2019.

[19] F. Miller, A. Vandome, and J. McBrewster, *Levenshtein Distance.* VDM Publishing, 2009.

[20] V. Romero-Gomez, A. Toselli, V. Bosch, J.-A. Sánchez, and E. Vidal, "Automatic alignment of handwritten images and transcripts for training handwritten text recognition systems," 04 2018, pp. 328–333.

[21] J. Sklansky, "Image segmentation and feature extraction," *IEEE Transactions on Systems, Man, and Cybernetics*, vol. 8, no. 4, pp. 237–247, 1978.

[22] M. Stenografförbundet, *Lärobok i Melins stenografi : Uppl. B / utg. av Melinska stenografförbundet.* Stockholm A.B Nordiska Bokhandeln, 1937.

[23] S. Sudholt and G. Fink, "Attribute cnns for word spotting in handwritten documents," *International Journal on Document Analysis and Recognition (IJDAR)*, vol. 21, 09 2018.

[24] S. Sudholt and G. A. Fink, "Phocnet: A deep convolutional neural network for word spotting in handwritten documents," 2017.

A   Appendix A

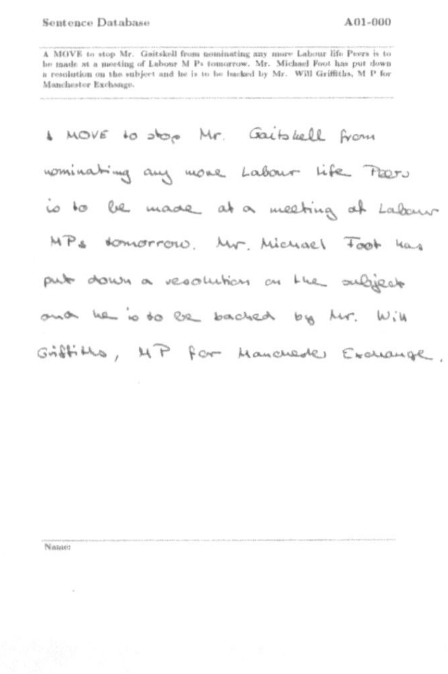

Figure 37 This image shows the page a01-000u from the IAM data set.

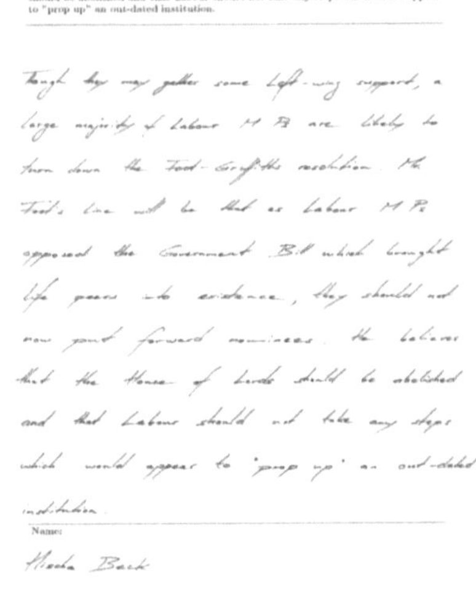

Figure 38 This image shows the page a01-003 from the IAM data set.

Sentence Database   A01-003

Though they may gather some Left-wing support, a large majority of Labour M Ps
are likely to turn down the Foot-Griffiths resolution. Mr. Foot's line will be that as
Labour M Ps opposed the Government Bill which brought life peers into existence,
they should not now put forward nominees. He believes that the House of Lords
should be abolished and that Labour should not take any steps which would appear
to "prop up" an out-dated institution.

Though they may gather some Left - wing
support, a large majority of Labour
MPs are likely to turn down the Foot -
Griffiths resolution. Mr. Foot's line will
be that as Labour MPs opposed the
Government Bill which brought life pears
into existence, they should not now put
forward nominees. He believes that the
House of Lords should be abolished and
that Labour should not take any steps
which would appear to "prop up" an out -

Name:

Figure 39 This image shows the page a01-003u from the IAM data set.

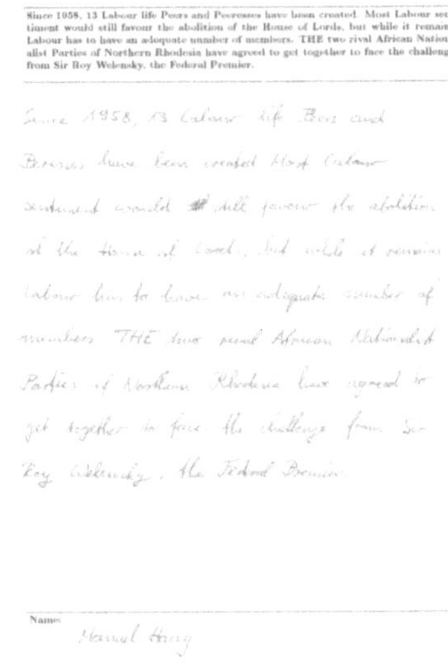

Sentence Database   A01-007

Since 1958, 13 Labour life Peers and Peeresses have been created. Most Labour sentiment would still favour the abolition of the House of Lords, but while it remains Labour has to have an adequate number of members. THE two rival African Nationalist Parties of Northern Rhodesia have agreed to get together to face the challenge from Sir Roy Welensky, the Federal Premier.

Figure 40 This image shows the page a01-007 from the IAM data set.

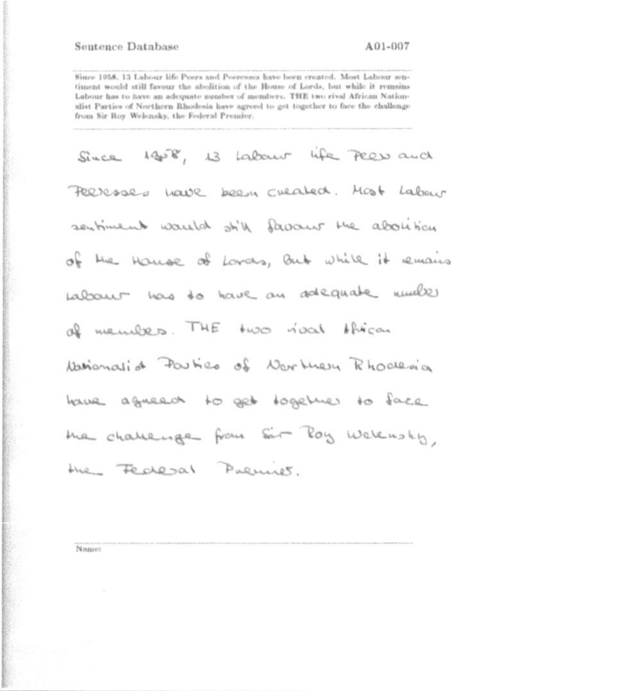

Sentence Database A01-007

Since 1958, 13 Labour life Peers and Peeresses have been created. Most Labour sentiment would still favour the abolition of the House of Lords, but while it remains Labour has to have an adequate number of members. THE two rival African Nationalist Parties of Northern Rhodesia have agreed to get together to face the challenge from Sir Roy Welensky, the Federal Premier.

Since 1958, 13 Labour life Peers and
Peeresses have been created. Most Labour
sentiment would still favour the abolition
of the House of Lords, but while it remains
Labour has to have an adequate number
of members. THE two rival African
Nationalist Parties of Northern Rhodesia
have agreed to get together to face
the challenge from Sir Roy Welensky,
the Federal Premier.

Name:

Figure 41 This image shows the page a01-007u from the IAM data set.

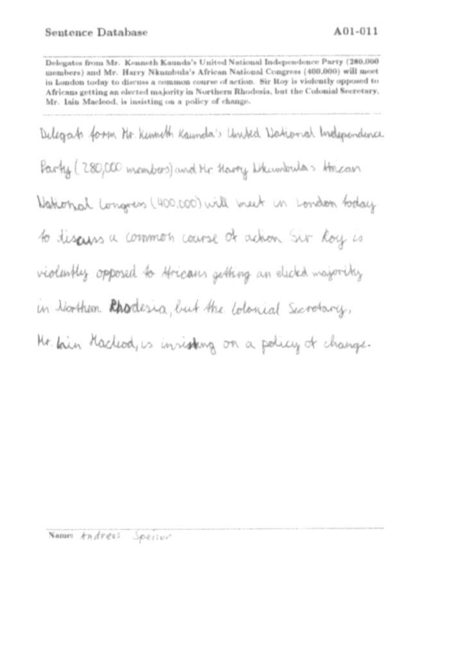

Sentence Database   A01-011

Delegates from Mr. Kenneth Kaunda's United National Independence Party (280,000 members) and Mr. Harry Nkumbula's African National Congress (400,000) will meet in London today to discuss a common course of action. Sir Roy is violently opposed to Africans getting an elected majority in Northern Rhodesia, but the Colonial Secretary, Mr. Iain Macleod, is insisting on a policy of change.

Delegates form Mr. Kenneth Kaunda's United National Independence Party (280,000 members) and Mr Harry Nkumbula's African National Congress (400,000) will meet in London today to discuss a common course of action Sir Roy is violently opposed to Africans getting an elected majority in Northern Rhodesia, but the Colonial Secretary, Mr. Iain Macleod, is insisting on a policy of change.

Name: Andreas Speiser

Figure 42 This image shows the page a01-011 from the IAM data set.

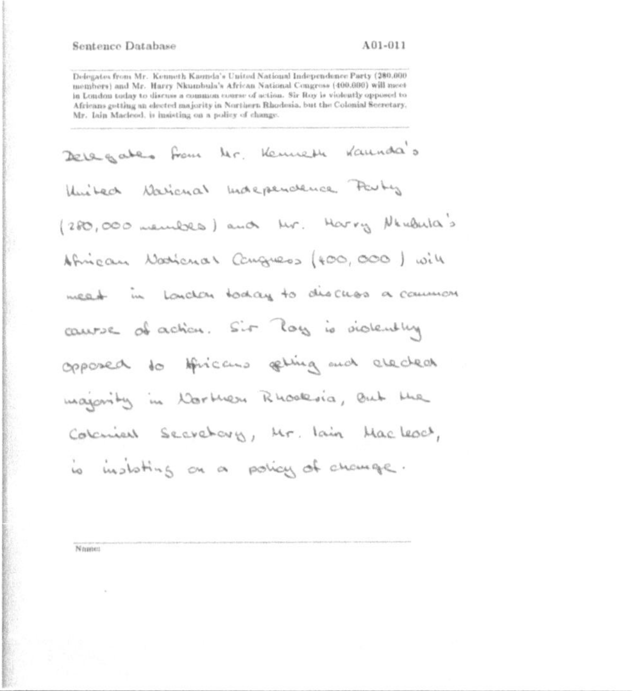

Sentence Database   A01-011

Delegates from Mr. Kenneth Kaunda's United National Independence Party (280,000 members) and Mr. Harry Nkumbula's African National Congress (400,000) will meet in London today to discuss a common course of action. Sir Roy is violently opposed to Africans getting an elected majority in Northern Rhodesia, but the Colonial Secretary, Mr. Iain Macleod, is insisting on a policy of change.

Delegates from Mr. Kenneth Kaunda's United National Independence Party (280,000 members) and Mr. Harry Nkumbula's African National Congress (400,000) will meet in London today to discuss a common course of action. Sir Roy is violently opposed to Africans getting and elected majority in Northern Rhodesia, but the Colonial Secretary, Mr. Iain Macleod, is insisting on a policy of change.

Name:

Figure 43 This image shows the page a01-011u from the IAM data set.

Sentence Database   A01-020

Mr. Macleod went on with the conference at Lancaster House despite the crisis
which had blown up. He has now revealed his full plans to the Africans and Liberals
attending. These plans do not give the Africans the overall majority they are seeking.
African delegates are studying them today. The conference will meet to discuss the
function of a proposed House of Chiefs.

Mr MacLeod went on with the conference at
Lancaster House despite the crisis which had
blown up. He has now revealed his full plans
to the Africans and Liberals attending. These
plans do not give the Africans the overall
majority they are seeking. African delegates
are studying them today. The conference
will meet to discuss the function of a
proposed House of Chiefs.

Name: Guido Kaufmann

Figure 44 This image shows the page a01-020 from the IAM data set.

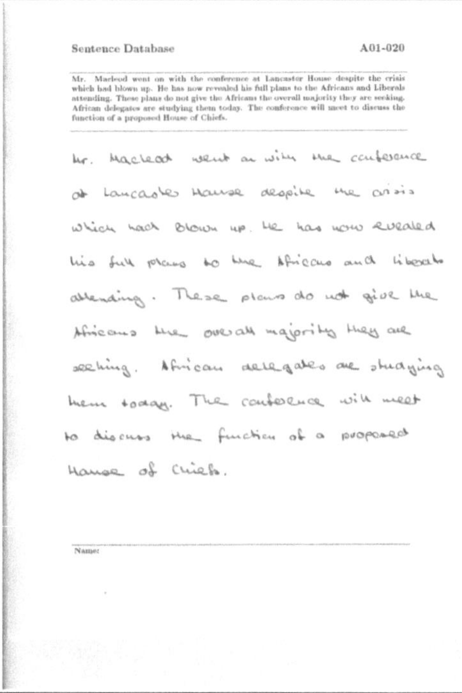

Sentence Database   A01-020

Mr. Macleod went on with the conference at Lancaster House despite the crisis which had blown up. He has now revealed his full plans to the Africans and Liberals attending. These plans do not give the Africans the overall majority they are seeking. African delegates are studying them today. The conference will meet to discuss the function of a proposed House of Chiefs.

Mr. Macleod went on with the conference at Lancaster House despite the crisis which had blown up. He has now revealed his full plans to the Africans and liberals attending. These plans do not give the Africans the overall majority they are seeking. African delegates are studying them today. The conference will meet to discuss the function of a proposed House of Chiefs.

Name:

Figure 45 This image shows the page a01-020u from the IAM data set.

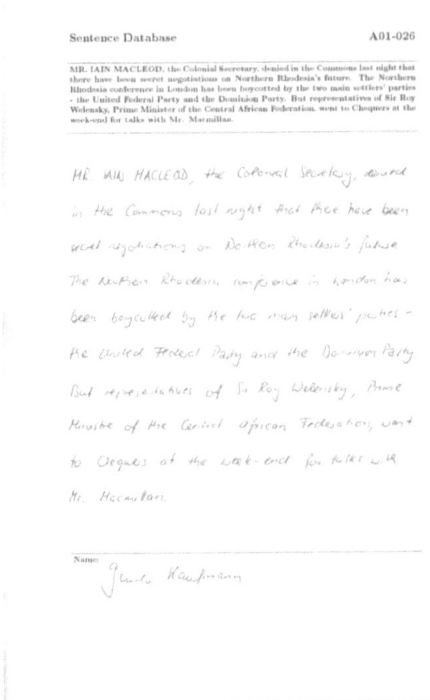

Sentence Database   A01-026

MR. IAIN MACLEOD, the Colonial Secretary, denied in the Commons last night that there have been secret negotiations on Northern Rhodesia's future. The Northern Rhodesia conference in London has been boycotted by the two main settlers' parties - the United Federal Party and the Dominion Party. But representatives of Sir Roy Welensky, Prime Minister of the Central African Federation, went to Chequers at the week-end for talks with Mr. Macmillan.

Figure 46 This image shows the page a01-026 from the IAM data set.

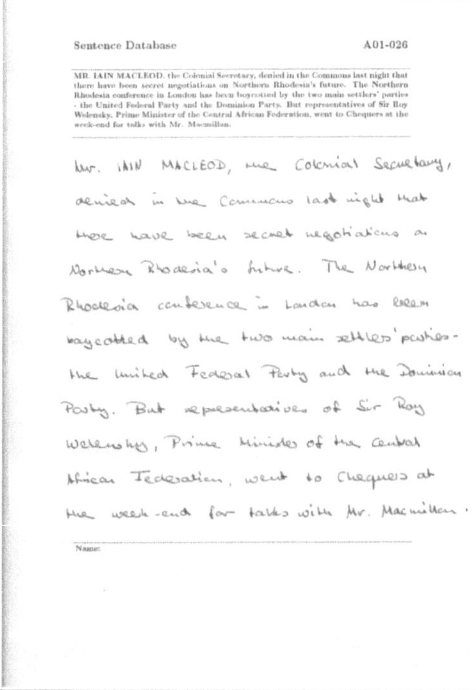

Sentence Database   A01-026

MR. IAIN MACLEOD, the Colonial Secretary, denied in the Commons last night that there have been secret negotiations on Northern Rhodesia's future. The Northern Rhodesia conference in London has been boycotted by the two main settlers' parties - the United Federal Party and the Dominion Party. But representatives of Sir Roy Welensky, Prime Minister of the Central African Federation, went to Chequers at the week-end for talks with Mr. Macmillan.

Mr. IAIN MACLEOD, the Colonial Secretary, denied in the Commons last night that there have been secret negotiations on Northern Rhodesia's future. The Northern Rhodesia conference in London has been boycotted by the two main settlers' parties - the United Federal Party and the Dominion Party. But representatives of Sir Roy Welensky, Prime Minister of the Central African Federation, went to Chequers at the week-end for talks with Mr. Macmillan.

Name:

Figure 47 This image shows the page a01-026u from the IAM data set.

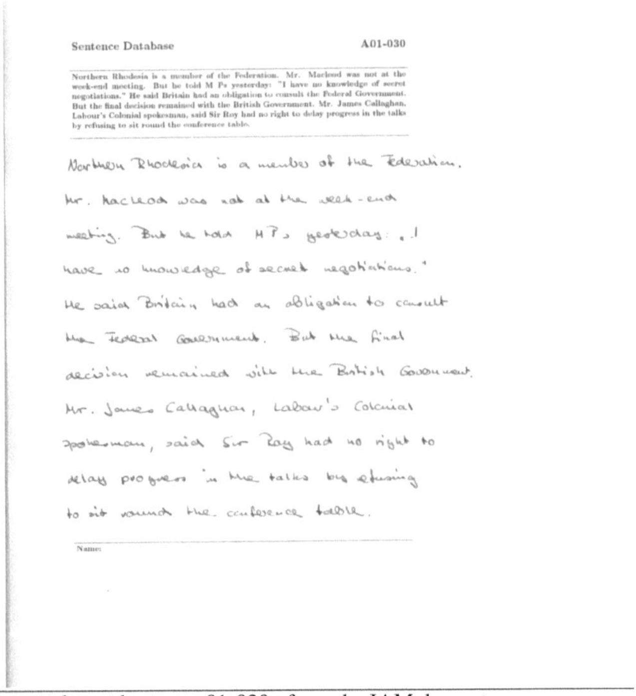

Sentence Database   A01-030

Northern Rhodesia is a member of the Federation. Mr. Macleod was not at the
week-end meeting. But he told M Ps yesterday: "I have no knowledge of secret
negotiations." He said Britain had an obligation to consult the Federal Government.
But the final decision remained with the British Government. Mr. James Callaghan,
Labour's Colonial spokesman, said Sir Roy had no right to delay progress in the talks
by refusing to sit round the conference table.

Northern Rhodesia is a member of the Federation.
Mr. Macleod was not at the week-end
meeting. But he told M Ps yesterday: "I
have no knowledge of secret negotiations."
He said Britain had an obligation to consult
the Federal Government. But the final
decision remained with the British Government.
Mr. James Callaghan, Labour's Colonial
spokesman, said Sir Roy had no right to
delay progress in the talks by refusing
to sit round the conference table.

Name:

Figure 48 This image shows the page a01-030u from the IAM data set.

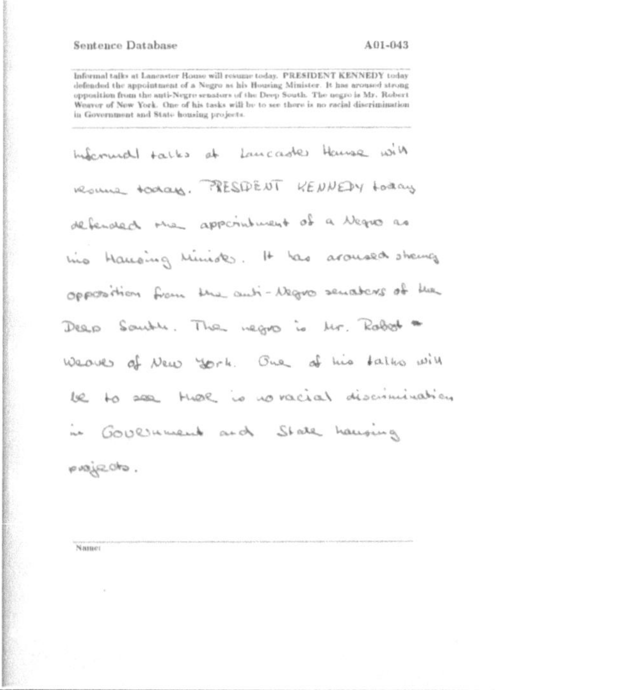

Sentence Database   A01-043

Informal talks at Lancaster House will resume today. PRESIDENT KENNEDY today
defended the appointment of a Negro as his Housing Minister. It has aroused strong
opposition from the anti-Negro senators of the Deep South. The negro is Mr. Robert
Weaver of New York. One of his tasks will be to see there is no racial discrimination
in Government and State housing projects.

Informal talks at Lancaster House will
resume today. PRESIDENT KENNEDY today
defended the appointment of a Negro as
his Housing Minister. It has aroused strong
opposition from the anti-Negro senators of the
Deep South. The negro is Mr. Robert
Weaver of New York. One of his talks will
be to see that is no racial discrimination
in Government and State housing
projects.

Name:

Figure 49 This image shows the page a01-043u from the IAM data set.

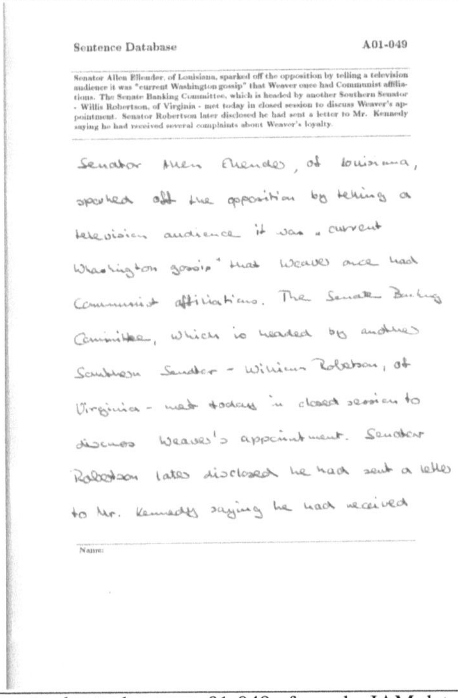

Sentence Database   A01-049

Senator Allen Ellender, of Louisiana, sparked off the opposition by telling a television audience it was "current Washington gossip" that Weaver once had Communist affiliations. The Senate Banking Committee, which is headed by another Southern Senator - Willis Robertson, of Virginia - met today in closed session to discuss Weaver's appointment. Senator Robertson later disclosed he had sent a letter to Mr. Kennedy saying he had received several complaints about Weaver's loyalty.

Senator Allen Ellender, of Louisiana, sparked off the opposition by telling a television audience it was "current Washington gossip" that Weaver once had Communist affiliations. The Senate Banking Committee, which is headed by another Southern Senator - Williams Robertson, of Virginia - met today in closed session to discuss Weaver's appointment. Senator Robertson later disclosed he had sent a letter to Mr. Kennedy saying he had received

Name:

Figure 50 This image shows the page a01-049u from the IAM data set.

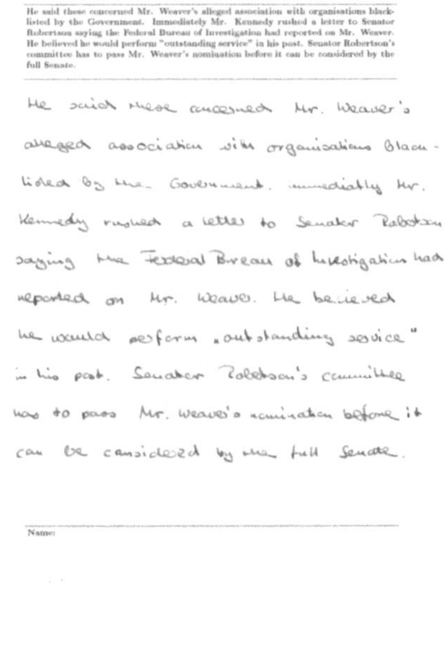

Sentence Database   A01-053

He said these concerned Mr. Weaver's alleged association with organisations black-
listed by the Government. Immediately Mr. Kennedy rushed a letter to Senator
Robertson saying the Federal Bureau of Investigation had reported on Mr. Weaver.
He believed he would perform "outstanding service" in his post. Senator Robertson's
committee has to pass Mr. Weaver's nomination before it can be considered by the
full Senate.

He said these concerned Mr. Weaver's alleged association with organisations Black-listed by the Government. Immediatly Mr. Kennedy rushed a letter to Senator Robertson saying the Federal Bureau of Investigation had reported on Mr. Weave. He believed he would perform "outstanding service" in his post. Senator Robertson's committee has to pass Mr. Weave's nomination before it can be considered by the full Senate.

Name:

Figure 51 This image shows the page a01-053u from the IAM data set.

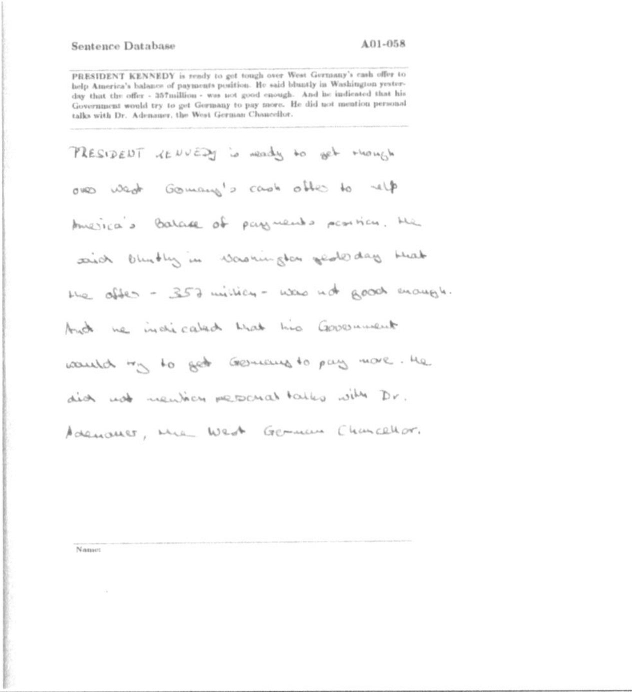

Sentence Database   A01-058

PRESIDENT KENNEDY is ready to get tough over West Germany's cash offer to help America's balance of payments position. He said bluntly in Washington yesterday that the offer - 357million - was not good enough. And he indicated that his Government would try to get Germany to pay more. He did not mention personal talks with Dr. Adenauer, the West German Chancellor.

PRESIDENT KENNEDY is ready to get tough

over West Germany's cash offer to help

America's Balance of payments position. He

said bluntly in Washington yesterday that

the offer - 357 million - was not good enough.

And he indicated that his Government

would try to get Germany to pay more. He

did not mention personal talks with Dr.

Adenauer, the West German Chancellor.

Name:

Figure 52 This image shows the page a01-058u from the IAM data set.

www.ingramcontent.com/pod-product-compliance
Lightning Source LLC
LaVergne TN
LVHW041734190726
843493LV00008B/2344